FROM OBAMA TO TRUMP

A Collection of Essays

Stewart T. Spencer

ISBN: 1541155025
ISBN 13: 9781541155022
Library of Congress Control Number: 2016921057
CreateSpace Independent Publishing Platform
North Charleston, South Carolina

ACTIONS SPEAK LOUDER
FEBRUARY 28, 2012

When he was running for president, good ol' Rick Perry managed to dodge this issue, but it still interests me: the governor is double-dipping Texas taxpayers by collecting his pension and his salary, too.

This is permitted by an obscure provision of Texas law that lets certain officials draw their state pensions without actually retiring. The law is made doubly obscure by a policy that personnel matters are secret. Ol' Rick 'fessed up, finally, when he declared for president and had to report to federal elections officials.

He says that lining his pockets is just a "common sense" use of a statute that has been on the books for years. What do you do if the money is there for the taking? You grab it and say nothing to the people you're fleecing unless you're forced to.

He calls this common sense. I call it greed and deceit. This from a man who dressed his candidacy in a pretense of higher values.

Perry no longer matters, but his example does. He has not been alone in approaching voters with the timeworn blandishment of Lotharios: Trust me. I'm different from the others.

But he wasn't different. He was just like anyone whose higher values are power and money. He reminds us that a smooth talker won't necessarily respect us in the morning. He reminds us that smooth talkers don't want listeners to ask too many questions.

This brings us to the smooth talk still being peddled in the Republican primaries. This may seem an odd way to characterize campaigns that daily set new standards for sheer vulgarity. But listen. The boys on the stump are peddling the oldest snake oil of all: Free lunch. Easy decisions. Simple answers.

The issues facing the country are not vexing and complex, don't you see? The decisions to be made are not daunting. Oh, no.

The issue facing the country is quite simple: the incumbent president is (choose your epithet) a boob, a scoundrel, a snob, a weakling, a power-hungry fiend, a secret Muslim, a secret secularist, a socialist, a Nazi, an uxorious puppet, a naïf, a foreigner.

And in the Republican primary, the central issue is really quite simple, don't you see? The other guy is a two-faced sharpie and a fool, to boot. An issue this simple requires only a simple decision by the voters: Trust me. I'm different from the others.

The Republican primaries have treated us to one dubious marvel after another. We have the ultra-right vamping on a theme popular with the sixties left: power to the people. (And never mind which people.) We have putative champions of limited government saying that private and personal matters should be opened to government influence. (Rick Santorum says the church should not be walled off from the state. By this he means, of course, that *his* church should not be walled off from the state.) Republican rhetoric these days radiates a genuine aversion to differences of opinion and a palpable fear that people with other views may prevail through the cunning tactic of voting in greater numbers.

There is nothing wrong with conservatism. Properly framed, it is an honorable tradition with worthwhile ideas on governance.

And there is reason aplenty to be wary of size and expense and intrusiveness in government.

But the offering from Republican candidates this year is not conservatism, and it is not heaven knows—a serious discussion of ends and means in governing a complex democracy. It is a dog's breakfast of pandering and posing. The candidates' "values" are costume jewelry chosen occasion by occasion.

Beneath their trumpeted differences, the Republican candidates have one very important thing in common. All are trying to persuade voters they can safely select a president without doing the work of making informed choices.

THIS JUST IN
MARCH 2, 2012

I don't watch much television news. There's too much show business in it for me. Even CNN has become infected. (Of the hucksters at Fox News, we need only say that P.T. Barnum would approve.)

In what follows I will display a prejudice or two. Let me begin by admitting it and by saying a few things that I think are nonetheless fair.

Every news medium has strengths and weaknesses. Print—my lifelong professional home—is deeper and more complete than the electronic types. But nowadays it is anachronistically slow. Also, alongside the Internet, it is no longer the best cafeteria in town. It no longer has the broadest menu.

Television is timely, easy to consume, and, heaven knows, ubiquitous. But TV is predisposed toward stories that can be told in pictures, and toward events—stuff that happens at specific times and places.

Elections are events that combine the bloviating extremes of electoral politics with the breathless, uptotheminuteeyewitnessalwaysonguard persona of TV news. One campaign or another always wants to inflate the importance of an election result. The TV cameras are always ready. The outcome can be darn near operatic. Consider the Iowa caucuses, where two-thirds fewer people voted than in my home county's last election for register of deeds.

Election nights can be a conspicuously mixed experience for reluctant viewers like me. The returns flow in at their own pace. But the alwaysonguard eyewitnesses have to be watching, watching, watching. Early in the evening of the Michigan primary, the anchors on two networks talked as much about the bells and whistles on their touch-screen displays as they did about the trickling returns. One anchor actually congratulated an analyst on his touch-screen form. (Who knew there were style points?)

I particularly enjoyed an early exchange that went this way:

Analyst: Governor Romney is doing well in parts of the state where he needs to do well if he's to win.
Anchor: Yes, if this trend continues, he'll be in good shape.
Translation: If Governor Romney keeps winning, he'll win.

At moments like those, I entertain a favorite fantasy (*prejudice alert!*). Two anchors gaze into the camera. He could be modeling men's grooming products. She looks like a refugee from the Stepford Wives.

She: Golly, Biff, we've been broadcasting for quite a while, but nothing is really happening yet.
He: Yes, Muffy, but we have air time to fill. I wonder if the viewers would like to see my vacation pictures.

My unkind image does touch on a serious point. Even the most prominent names in television news may talk a lot without actually saying anything. Instead they hold a mirror up to others. If those others are babbling and dissembling, the result accentuates the essential shallowness of the medium. Thus we have a year in which some of TV's most incisive political commentary is being delivered outside the news shows—by comedians.

Meanwhile, important stories unfold that are not so easily told in pictures and are not focused in a discrete event. One of this year's big ones has so far been little noted: In the aggregate, turnout in the Republican primaries has been low. A big verdict has been delivered by people who voted with their feet—or, more precisely, with their buns, by keeping them couch-bound on election day. A lot of folks have declined to attend the circus.

All this being said, the American electorate tends to be pretty level-headed over an expanse of time—which is the terrain on which democracy works. Voters don't take all their information from campaigning politicians, through whatever medium. They form their views from a much larger set of considerations. (I think people paid attention while House Speaker John Boehner and the other Big Men on Campus were hazing the freshman Obama. Americans don't like bullies. I'm curious to see how much they'll remember in November.)

So, the campaigns will continue to dispirit a lot of us.

Television news will continue to annoy me.

The Republic will survive.

But I do wish Wolf Blitzer could go ten minutes without telling me I'm in the Situation Room.

LOOKING IN THE MIRROR
MARCH 5, 2012

We need not linger over Rush Limbaugh, the radio personality who used the airwaves to savage a private citizen for trying to exercise a citizen's rights. Limbaugh and his niche audience like to portray him as a commentator. But he is in fact just an entertainer of an especially low sort. Having said that he is the political equivalent of a pornographer, we've said enough and should move on.

We should move on to the context and the aftermath of the Limbaugh incident. In both there is occasion for sadness, concern, and a strong dose of self-examination.

At issue was the posture of public policy toward insurance coverage for contraception. Sandra Fluke, a Georgetown University law student, wanted to testify before a congressional hearing. In her view, contraception is an essential form of health care for many women. She feels government should not limit access for doctrinal reasons having nothing to do with public health.

Republicans maneuvered to prevent her from speaking. Democrats gave her an alternative forum. Limbaugh called her a variety of vulgar names on the air.

In a libel on conservatism, Limbaugh purports to speak for conservatives. But Republican presidential candidates responded to his vicious outburst with slow and tepid criticism. The office of House Speaker John Boehner issued a craven statement. Other Republicans in Congress were notably silent.

The context is an enduring preoccupation on the political right with matters of sex and reproduction. It produces—often on the issue of abortion—attempts to write religious precept into civil law. This is both an affront to our country's foremost principles and a remarkably shortsighted approach to governance. Once the door is opened to government enforcement of religion, any religious interest group with enough votes can use the access thus afforded. Christian conservatives are not well advised to bet on long-term dominance for their point of view.

(And in answer to one question implicit in the above, let me say that I have my own reservations about abortion. I just don't want the government enforcing my personal values on my neighbors.)

Other concerns are stirred by the attempt of congressional Republicans in this episode to prevent the expression of views unlike their own. The government of the United States is supposed to shelter, respect, and mediate among varying opinions and interests. But nowadays government may be a mere instrument of power for the voting bloc of the moment. The rampant partisanship in Congress is a fundamental betrayal of principle and public trust.

For the past couple of years, we've seen it in the attempts of a willful Republican minority to sabotage the work of a duly elected president. We've seen it in political brinksmanship that brought the country to the verge of economic chaos. We've seen it in relentless attempts to shackle the government of all the people to the personal views of some of the people.

Noteworthy in this connection is the recent announcement by Maine Republican moderate Olympia Snowe that she won't seek reelection to the Senate. She cites long service, yes, but also unwillingness to invest any more of her life in an institution that does not reliably attend to its higher purposes.

"I do not believe," she wrote in the *Washington Post*, "that in the near term the Senate can correct itself from within...But whenever Americans have set our minds to tackling enormous problems, we have met with tremendous success. I am convinced that, if the people of our nation raise their collective voices, we can effect a renewal of the art of legislating—and restore the luster of a Senate that still has the potential of achieving monumental solutions to our nation's most urgent challenges. I look forward to helping the country raise those voices to support the Senate returning to its deserved status and stature—but from outside the institution."

Senator Snowe is saying, with elevated tact, that Congress behaves badly in part because the public tolerates it. Many Americans don't vote or bother to inform themselves on important issues. Their neglect magnifies the power of the active few.

To paraphrase that erstwhile political sage Pogo Possum, if we look very far for malefactors in this situation, we'll find ourselves. The profile we see in the worst face of Congress is our own.

GAY MARRIAGE
MARCH 6, 2012

I am a believing Christian, an avid reader of the Bible, and a pro-
ponent of gay marriage.

Let's begin with the Bible. Formally, and on my own, I have
studied it for twenty-five years. It is a warm, wise, earthy, wonderfully sophisticated book. It is not like the caricatures made of it by
rule-mongering moralizers.

In parts it is a marvel of literature. Consider just one example:
how would you capture on paper a fall from innocent grace to
worldly shame? Genesis accomplishes this in just seven words ad-
dressed by God to Adam and Eve when he finds them attempting
clothing: "Who told you that you were naked?"

I read the Bible frequently and cherish it as a source of nourishment. I see in it no requirement that we condemn homosexuality out of hand. Explaining would require far more than a blog
posting. For now let me simply say that this is what I find in my
study. This also is what I am told by the clergy of the church I

attend and leaders of the denomination we belong to. (I am an Episcopalian.) The Bible that I read calls upon me to respect the dignity of every human being, to love others and not to judge them.

Over the years I have acquired several gay friends. I have a couple of gay relatives. With the single exception of their sexual orientation, they are like my straight friends and relatives. Most are exemplary people. Some are flawed. They work, pay taxes, give to charity, go to church. They love their families and keep good homes. They care about the difference between right and wrong. Some are committed in long-term, monogamous relationships. For some, relationships have failed. Some prefer to remain single. In short, they live life as it comes to the rest of us, and they harm no one in greater degree than all of us do.

It is simply not true to say that gay people threaten proper values or the stability of families. Homosexuality is not contagious, and neither is it inherently hostile to principled behavior. I see no reason why my gay friends should not have the same right as I to make a marital commitment. I see no reason why the government should set out to prevent it.

Alas, members of my state legislature do not agree. Although gay marriage is already against the law in North Carolina, the legislature has proposed a double prohibition in the form of an amendment to the state constitution. The proposal will go to the voters in May.

The debate has played out along familiar lines. Proponents cite a Biblical standard of right and wrong—as they define it. Opponents say gay marriage is an issue of civil rights, not religion.

I say the issue, as it is framed in this proposal for a constitutional amendment, is some of both.

Gay marriage is an issue of civil rights insofar as a minority is arbitrarily barred from doing what the majority freely does. But in North Carolina, in May, it will also be a religious issue in this way:

the proposed amendment represents an attempt to write religious precept into civil law.

This is a ghastly and dangerous mistake. Moreover, it is an attempt to write into civil law one particular interpretation of Christian scripture, to the exclusion of others.

This is offensive to me, as a Christian, on religious grounds. I read the Bible. I have read all of it twice, most of it three times, and the New Testament more times than I can count. I have studied it with experts and with teachers of palpable spirituality. I know what it says and what it does not say. I know that it can be approached from different directions and experienced in different ways. I know that the heart of its profound beauty is its capacity to touch all of us, no matter who we are or where we are in life.

I don't want the legislature of North Carolina telling me what I am allowed to hear in it.

LAUGH A LITTLE, CRY A LITTLE
MARCH 10, 2012

I n this season of political comedy—some intentional, some not—
I think of earlier humorists who've commented on life, human
nature, and our shared lot as a nation.

Archy the cockroach was created in 1916 by New York journalist and author Don Marquis. Archy and his friend Mehitabel the
alley cat came into the newsroom after hours to talk about this 'n'
that. Archy wrote things down, sometimes in verse, by jumping
on the keys of a typewriter (remember those?). Archy couldn't use
capital letters, because it was physically impossible for him to hold
down the shift key and a letter key at the same time.

Marquis and his friends left us a variety of pithy sayings. One in
particular may resonate with some folks today: "When a man tells
you he got rich through hard work, ask him: 'Whose?'"

Irish barkeep Mr. Dooley was created around the turn of the
century by Chicago journalist Finley Peter Dunne. Mr. Dooley

approached life with a wary eye and a ready quip. He is the one who famously said, "Trust everybody but cut the cards."

He also said that the mission of newspapers was to "comfort the afflicted and afflict the comfortable." The quote was later adopted by several religious leaders, including one archbishop of Canterbury, who said it described the mission of the church. Has any other image migrated so far from its roots?

Mr. Dooley is perhaps best remembered for saying, "Politics ain't beanbag." In his Chicago, then as now, politics were not for the faint of heart. But the notion has broader pertinence, as we have seen over the past few months.

The Republicans have held the spotlight so far. We could say their search for a presidential nominee has maintained the decorum of a soccer riot, except that a soccer riot displays greater clarity of purpose and method.

Mitt Romney has wanted for years to be president but still struggles to explain why. Rick Santorum seems to think the presidency is a position in a religious order.

The aim of Ron Paul's little campaign is mysterious, unless he hopes through sheer persistence to create a niche for amiable crackpots.

Newt Gingrich wants (as ever) what Newt wants, and devil take the hindmost.

While the Republicans' extended train wreck saves comedy writers a lot of work, it is not a happy development for the nation. Well into a presidential election year, we have heard nothing resembling a fully formed discussion of the decisions facing the country. The Republican candidates have largely settled for calling each other boobs and scoundrels. Those who've occasionally peeked above their fray have directed the same kind of twaddle at President Obama.

The spectacle must especially disappoint people who value the contributions thoughtful conservatism can make to governance.

They may remember a time when conservative politicians could have dignity and substance. If Don Marquis were alive to assess today's Republican candidates, he might say again: "An idea is not responsible for those who believe it."

Among humorists I've always liked Will Rogers, the cowboy sage of the twenties and thirties. He could be funny and dispense a kind of prairie wisdom at the same time. Ol' Will once said, "Everything is changing. People are taking their comedians seriously, and the politicians as a joke."

I guess he was smiling when he said it. He usually did.

In any case, he's probably looking down on us now and considering that things haven't changed so much after all.

ODDS 'N' ENDS
MARCH 15, 2012

He was an older guy—late sixties by the look of him. She was about the same age. Dressed for a Sunday stroll, they were holding hands on a downtown street corner and waiting for a light to change.

A pesky breeze was cold, but the day was pretty to look at. Late winter sunlight made bold shadows on the pavement.

He leaned over and gave her a kiss on the temple. It was a small one, but more than a peck. She turned to smile up at him.

A matron in a passing car saw the exchange and beamed.

There are still nice people all around us.

＊＊＊

I enjoy college sports. The men's national basketball tournament is a special treat for me. The game at its best can have balletic grace.

But as I watch, I wonder: when do some of these young men become the preening thugs who are too plentiful in professional sports?

They start at an early age, I fear. In our culture, we teach 'em young that athletes are not subject to the same standards of behavior as the rest of us.

⊫ ⊨

My grandson just celebrated his third birthday. He is a precious child whose laughter gives me a stab of the sweetest heartache you can imagine.

The same is true of my granddaughter. She's just a little younger than he is.

Both my grandchildren have the bright, settled countenances of children who are well and skillfully loved. Yes, getting a good start in life takes a bit of luck, with mental and physical health and such. But beyond that is the particular blessing of kids who know that they are cherished in a proper way. You can see it, I think, in the way they bear themselves—in their posture toward the world.

In this demeanor, my grandchildren remind me of another little boy who crosses my path from time to time. He's also about three. He is a bright-eyed, curious, chatty youngster. He radiates a feeling that his world makes sense, that he is happy and secure in it.

He breaks into a huge grin when he sees his parents approaching.

They are a lesbian couple.

Why not?

⊫ ⊨

Senator John McCain is tetchy about the way he and Sarah Palin are portrayed in a new movie. It is said to be particularly hard on her.

He insists she was the "best qualified" person to be his running mate in the presidential election of 2008.

Reminds me of another writer's comment that McCain has become the crazy uncle in Washington's attic.

Air travel is on my agenda this year. The prospect already has me in a bad mood. Flying nowadays is like getting mugged: they treat you badly, and they take your money, too.

I can remember when airplanes flew on time. As a veteran consumer of the standard variety of goods and services, I can remember when the basic concept of customer service was alive outside the history books.

No more. Take those automated phone trees, for example. They are a bane (especially the ones featuring assurances that my phone call is important to the people who can't get around to answering it.) We undertook this week to redeem some of those bonus points the credit card companies are so proud of. The exercise eventually involved two telephone attempts, three e-mails, a bout of head-scratching, some helpless listening to recorded information we didn't want, and—finally—conversations with people who read from a script. I have negotiated mortgages with less trouble.

Customer service has been significantly impeded by computers. All of us have waited, and waited, and waited, while some poor clerk at the other end of a commercial transaction said, "I'm sorry for the delay. Our computers have been very slow today."

Some days, mine is slow, too. It has a mind of its own. It is especially willful when the virus protection software takes control and grinds through an extended search for the latest mutations of electronic vermin.

The protection is beneficial, of course. I just don't like being bitch-slapped by a machine.

And so aging has given me one more opportunity to eat my words. I always swore I wouldn't be one of those fuddy-duddies who complain that things are not like they used to be.

But they're not.

And I don't like it.

So there.

UNCLE BARLOW
MARCH 17, 2012

I got a letter from Uncle Barlow the other day. He writes from time to time.

I should explain that he isn't necessarily my uncle at all. His branch of the family tree is way out on the fringes, and I'm not clear on our exact relationship. The closest I ever got to an explanation was from a guy at a family reunion. He said Uncle Barlow was my mother's third cousin's second husband. That may be true, or the guy may have been brushing me off. He was eager to get to the flask he'd stashed in the azaleas behind the picnic shelter.

Also, "Uncle Barlow" may not actually be Uncle Barlow's name. He lives out in the country among people who've been there for generations. A lot of them are tagged with the Barlow name one way or another. Even the county is named Barlow. So while it's possible that "Barlow" is part of Uncle Barlow's proper name, it's also possible that it's just a sort of handle, like Minnesota Fats or Memphis Slim or Cincinnati Kid.

Uncle Barlow has been retired for years. He spends his days whittling and watching what he calls "the passing parade of life." If the parade begins to move too fast for him, he writes me. Here's what 's been on his mind lately:

Dear Nephew,

[He calls me "nephew." I just go with it.]

I read in the Barlow Clarion that this fellow Rick Santorum is beginning to do pretty good in that election the Republicans are having. This has me concerned and confused, because it looks to me like if he became president he'd want to make us all go to church and have a lot of children.

Now, I always thought that church was one thing, and the government was something else. But I never did very good in school, so maybe I just didn't understand. I'll keep working on that part.

And I think I'm OK on the business about having a lot of kids, what with my dear Beulah being gone all these years. Nowadays there are only four single women my age in Barlow County. Three of them are in the home, and the fourth one is the Widow Cumbee. If Mr. Santorum ever saw the widow Cumbee, I think he'd be willing to give me a pass.

What's really got me stirred up is this church thing. I've never been much of a church fellow, so most of what I know is second-hand. But I do notice some things. For example, take the folks who swarm down to the First Barlow Church on Sundays. I notice that during the week they don't exactly practice what they preach, you might say.

This must be OK with Mr. Santorum, as I read in the Clarion that he did some of the same sort of thing when he was up there in the U.S. Senate. From time to time he'd say one thing and then vote the other way. I guess he had examples to follow, since a lot of them seem to do it in the Congress. That's according to what I read in the Clarion, anyway. I wonder if they give newcomers some kind of training class when they arrive, so they don't look clumsy the first few times they double back on their word.

I've never had any such training, so I struggle with the notion of saying you believe something and then acting like you really never did. I tried it for a few hours last Tuesday, and it made my head swim. Maybe if Mr. Santorum gets elected he can make Congress offer classes to everybody.

About those fellows Ron Paul and Newt Gingrich I don't know what to think. Judging from the way they're lagging behind, others don't either. Why they keep running is a mystery to me. Maybe they just enjoy having friends pay for their travel.

Now, this Romney fellow seems to be an interesting kind of bird. I read in the Clarion that he just changes what he says he believes to fit the situation he's in. This doesn't seem to me like the best way to behave, but I guess it's convenient.

It reminds me of what happened here last winter with the youngster in the devil suit.

Some fraternity boys over the college had a bunch of new pledges they needed to break in. They dressed them in all different kinds of costumes and left them out in the country to get back the best way they could. The one they dropped off here in Barlow County had on a devil costume.

He soon got lost and wandered around until after dark. He began to get pretty scared. When he saw lights and heard voices over at the First Barlow Church, he made right for it.

Inside, they were having a revival meeting. It had lasted into the night, because they had one of those guest preachers who can talk so long you need a haircut by the time he's done. He was reaching full roar about hellfire and damnation when the back door of the church flew open, and in staggered the college boy in the devil suit. He was so scared his eyes were bugging out. And it was a cold night, so his breath was all smoky in the air.

People took one look at that sight and began diving for the doors and windows. The Widow Cumbee doesn't miss any meals, so it can take her an extra little while to move. By the time she got all of herself under way, most of the exits were busy. She decided to make for the back door of the church. All the commotion had scared the college boy even worse than he already was, and he decided to scamper out the same way. The two of them got jammed up in the doorway, belly to belly and eyeball to eyeball. The Widow Cumbee commenced to shouting, "Look here! I want you to know I've really been on your side all along!"

I don't think the Widow Cumbee is likely to run for president, but judging from events lately you never can tell what kind of folks might volunteer.

Sincerely,

Your Uncle Barlow

A TANGLED WEB
MARCH 21, 2012

I got another letter from Uncle Barlow the other day. He is stirred up about public affairs of one sort and another. Here's his view of things from way out in the countryside.

Dear Nephew,

We have a situation here in Barlow County. Oh, my goodness do we have a situation.

The Widow Cumbee is sweet on Floyd over at the grain elevator, hardware store and auto repair. She looks at him like that Callista Gingrich looks at her man Newt.

Floyd encouraged her at first, but then he started wishing he hadn't. Things came to a head when he took her to a double feature at the Starlite Drive In. She got carried away when the cuddling commenced, and Floyd came home with a cracked rib and second thoughts. He keeps trying to wiggle away from her, but she's too moonstruck to notice.

He hasn't been in a crack like this since he told his late wife he had the green apple quickstep and skipped her family reunion to go fishing. Floyd caught a lunker that day. Biggest fish he ever landed. He wanted ever so bad to brag about it, but of course he didn't dare, because he'd lied to his wife about spending all day on the thunder mug. He finally gave the fish to Scooter over at the cafe. But he made Scooter tell people he never would have caught it if Floyd hadn't taught him how.

Anyhow, Floyd gets in trouble when he flimflams people about his true outlook. Millie over at the library says that's what Rick Santorum is doing, by the way. He's another one of those fellows who's running for president. Nowadays he wears suits and talks about foreign policy and such. A while back, before he started getting more votes, he wore a sweater vest and talked a lot about sex. He's against birth control, to mention just one thing, and not only for himself. He's against it for everybody. He talked and talked about it. He talked so much about it that finally his own wife started saying maybe he should change the subject.

Millie says that now he's posing and pretending. She says that, back when he started out, he was trying to look like the kind of fellow who might help you jump start your car, but that now he's trying to look presidential. I said maybe his sweater vest is at the dry cleaners. Millie just snorted. She says that all the women are going to vote against him. She says he wants a "theocracy." And it certainly does look to me like he's apt to go beyond preaching and get to meddling.

That fellow Mitt Romney doesn't suit Millie any better. He's been complaining about gas prices. Millie said she would, too, if her spouse drove two Cadillacs. And then there's the business about light bulbs. Romney said President Obama and his folks "banned" the light bulbs everybody's used all these years. But the trouble is, that's just not true. Millie showed me in back issues of *The Barlow Clarion* how this notion of switching to more efficient light bulbs got started under the last President Bush and was passed by big votes of both parties in Congress.

I said I hoped a presidential candidate wouldn't just flat-out lie. I said maybe Romney just got confused. Millie said who wants a president who can't keep light bulbs straight. She has a sharp tongue, sometimes.

Anyhow, back to Floyd and the Widow Cumbee. She just won't leave him alone. Floyd has started inventing excuses for laying out of work at the elevator and store, so he won't be so easy for her to find.

Trouble is, Floyd is the only person who knows right where everything is in the store. They're still using the inventory system old Mr. Flack set up in 1960. And since he kept the system all up in his head, and since he turned up his toes a couple of years ago, shopping for hardware or auto parts has come to be a time-consuming thing if Floyd isn't there.

Word got around town that things weren't just right at the store, and business went soft. The business reporter and society columnist at *The Clarion* says this has set off "economic ripples" in town. The story didn't come right out and say it's all because the Widow Cumbee wants Floyd to service her transmission, but everybody already knows that, so there was no need to dwell on it.

The situation has also caused personal problems for people. Scooter's wife sent him to buy a tack hammer so he could hang some little pictures in their living room. When the folks at the store just couldn't find one, Scooter tried to use a ball peen hammer, and he made an egg-sized hole in the dry wall.

Now, Scooter's wife is one of those people with a powerful need to be unhappy. She can find personal issues in a dinner menu. When she is presented with an opportunity as real as a hole in the dry wall, she really goes to town. She has cut off all communication inside their house, if you get my meaning.

So, as I said, we have a situation here in Barlow County. There's talk of forming a citizens committee to press upon Floyd an obligation to step up and do right by the Widow Cumbee. We all have our civic duty, even in our sex lives.

That's what Rick Santorum says.

Sincerely,

Your Uncle Barlow

HATRED AND THE LAW
MARCH 26, 2012

W e are all shaped by the experiences of our youth. I spent part of mine in areas where the races were segregated by law.

I remember it as a source of anxiety and confusion. My grandmother's housekeeper, who became a beloved mother figure to me, came and went only through the back door because she was black. I was admonished by ostensibly good-hearted adults that black people were genetically inferior and that it was unfair or even cruel to expect them to bear the full burdens of citizenship. I couldn't understand how all the values 1 was otherwise taught could be inverted on the issue of race.

Years later we moved up north, and I learned why one writer called it the Piety Belt. There I found Jim Crow living quite comfortably, albeit in subtler disguise. To this day I remember our town as the most thoroughly segregated community I have ever seen. My friends and neighbors sheltered in the notion that racism was peculiar to the American South and that it was therefore someone else's problem. It required of them no personal examination of behavior or conscience. Not a whit. And it received none.

Jim's disguises would later be penetrated. One of the nastiest school desegregation battles in the country's history was fought in Boston. Segregation of the Philadelphia public schools was contested for years—in the City of Brotherly Love. Fear, frustration, and anger among African Americans erupted in cities of every region.

Fast forward to the present. Is America a better place on issues of race? Yes. Is it the kind of place we ought to want? No. As a national columnist reminded us just last week, bias still is "sadly, embedded in American culture."

Events remind us as well. The "N" word remains a red flag for violent boobs—and for some of them, a license to kill. Last year a group of white teens in Mississippi sought out a black stranger and murdered him for sport. They joked about it over burgers afterward. They were, of course, people of a certain sort. But unless they came from Mars, they were nourished by a climate of attitude toward race.

The climate is manifest in other ways and in other places. The New York City police department is today being credibly accused of racial profiling. The charge is so widely leveled at law enforcement that no sentient American above the age of ten needs an explanation of the phrase "driving while black." Elements of the immigration debate are tinged with racial hostility. So is some of the vitriol directed at the president of the United States.

Bigotry is not limited to matters of race, of course. The form specifically on the mind of that national columnist was homophobia. And he was making an odd argument. He said the Rutgers student convicted of committing hate crimes against his gay roommate should not have been prosecuted.

The details are both sordid and grim. Dharun Ravi videotaped his roommate, Tyler Clementi, in a sexual encounter with another man. Ravi then invited other people to watch the video. He tweeted that Clementi was gay. Soon afterward, Clementi committed suicide. Ravi now faces prison and deportation to his native India.

The columnist, a law professor, wrote in part:

[L]egally speaking, Ravi did not cause the death, nor was it reasonably foreseeable. Of the millions of people who are bullied or who suffer invasions of privacy, few kill themselves...

For his stupidity, Ravi should be shamed by his fellow students and kicked out of his dorm, but he should not be sent to prison for years and then banished from the United States

The problem with broad (hate crime) laws like New Jersey's is that they come too close to punishing people for what they think. Bigotry, including homophobia, is morally condemnable, but in a free country it should not be a punishable offense...

Ravi did not invent homophobia, but he is being scapegoated for it. Bias against gay people is, sadly, embedded in American culture. Until last year, people were kicked out of the military because they were homosexuals.

These notions might suffice if life were a matter of nicely balanced abstractions. But it isn't. In real life, certain attitudes can do real harm.

Homophobia mimics racism in holding that some people are not worth a full measure of respect. And it can reach ghastly extremes. In 1998, gay college student Matthew Shepard was tortured and murdered in an incident so notorious that a federal hate crime statute bears his name. My newspaper last Sunday told the story of Calvin Burdine, sentenced to death in 1984 for the Texas murder of his male partner: "Burdine's court-appointed lawyer, when not dozing, referred to his client as a 'fairy.' The prosecutor, meanwhile, demanded the death penalty by arguing that gays actually look forward to the rewards of prison life." (The death sentence was later reversed.)

Homophobia widely takes forms that are less dangerous but still offensive to a proper sense of right and wrong. A friend with a gay pride sticker on his bumper learned to ignore the occasional shout of "faggot" as he used the public streets. (Let us note the shouters' assumption that heterosexuals within earshot would not mind.) Several gay friends have told me over the years of being ostracized in their own neighborhoods. As recently as the 1970s, a Hollywood bar and grill featured matchbook covers that said "Faggots stay out." The plain fact is this: in our culture, gay people are routinely the targets of disdain, abuse, discrimination, and worse.

In this climate, Ravi cannot—or should not—have failed to imagine that Clementi would feel threatened. Did Ravi cause the suicide? No one will ever know. Was his behavior worse than merely juvenile and stupid? Yes, it was.

Any notion that some people are worth less than others is insidious and dangerous. I saw it legally inflicted on black people in my youth. It remains a fixture in American race relations today. As our columnist notes above, until last year it was embedded in the policies of the United States government.

Hate crime statutes draw a fine line, yes. But it's an important one. As in the case of Ravi and Clementi, people who pour gasoline on embers can rightly be held accountable for what happens next. American citizens should not have to fear their neighbors—or their roommates.

HIGH ROAD, LOW ROAD
APRIL 4, 2012

In one scene of the movie *Game Change*, which dramatizes the McCain/Palin presidential campaign of 2008, the John McCain character is campaigning in close quarters with his audience. He has handed his microphone to a woman who declares her support for him by heaping personal invective on then-senator Barack Obama.

The McCain character is startled and troubled. He feels he should demur. In the middle of her rant, he gently takes the microphone away from her and says (I am paraphrasing), "No ma'am, he is none of those things. He is a good, honorable man with whom I happen to disagree."

The scene invites us to consider how far we've descended into politics of sneer and insult. Invective has followed Obama into the White House. And now the Republican presidential primaries have tested our collective gag reflex.

There is precedent, alas. The second President Bush was routinely vilified and ridiculed. In fact, the tactic of personal attack has waxed and waned throughout the country's political history. But as citizens we can only deal with the issues of our own times, and we have reached extremes we should want to correct.

To my ear, the tone of discourse began to sour in the 1960s, with objections to the Vietnam War. Opponents went from calling the war a terrible mistake—which it surely was—to calling it "immoral." This was a short step from saying that policymakers who favored the war were themselves immoral people. The step was soon taken.

Easy notions are infectious. It is seductively easy to say that people who disagree with us are deficient by virtue of their disagreement. We don't have to grapple with contending ideas. We don't have to do the work of tolerance.

When political opinions thus become dogma, something is lost in the conversation of democracy. Respectful disagreement is an early casualty. Factions want their way, and they want it now, because their way is the one true way. Differing opinions are to be vanquished. Opponents are enemies.

It is natural for me to believe that my opinions are superior to yours; however, I should not demand that you believe it, too. Nor should I expect the government to demand it of you on my behalf. The American political system is not supposed to choose a master ideology for the country. It is supposed to mediate among the varied ideologies that should be safe among us.

This principle does not suit dogmatic politics; they foster single-issue extremes. Witness attempts to write religious precepts into civil law on issues of abortion and gay marriage. They license officeholders to slight a duty to serve all the people. Witness efforts by a willful Republican minority in Congress to sabotage the work of a duly elected President Obama. (At the same time, in a particularly sharp irony, doctrinaire voices in the left wing of his own party scold the president for being less liberal than they are. In this they ignore that the American electorate is less liberal than they are.)

Our political system is intended to permit or even force differing opinions to work together. Dogmatic politics are impatient with the very idea, and impatience is by nature disrespectful of its object.

Being thus ill-equipped for the better vocabulary of the system, dogmatic politics lapse into their own. The whole point of discussion is subverted. Invective does what invective always does: it camouflages a bankruptcy of useful language.

The politics of sneer and insult are offensive in being vulgar. They are deplorable in being empty of legitimate public purpose.

OBAMA AND THE COURT
APRIL 11, 2012

News item:
President Barack Obama said "Good morning" to a marine guard in the White House today.

The president's comment was sharply criticized by Republican presidential candidates past and present; Tea Party legislators and their extended families; House Speaker John Boehner and his tanning coach; and also by Clint Eastwood, Wayne Newton, Kid Rock, Larry the Cable Guy, and Willy the Dolphin.

Well, OK. Things are not really as bad as all that. But sometimes folks do get close to begrudging the president his own words. The latest dustup involves the Supreme Court's review of the new national health-care law. President Obama said in a news conference he was confident of the law's constitutionality. He said that for the court to find otherwise would, in his opinion, require it to reach into inappropriate judicial activism.

This excited Senate Republican leader Mitch McConnell, who said the comments "crossed a dangerous line." He advised the president to "back off."

I will borrow a phrase and call this pious baloney. (See the collected sayings of Newt Gingrich.)

Tussles between the judiciary and other branches of government are not new. An early sally came from the Supreme Court itself in 1803. Before then, the power of the court to overturn acts of Congress had been considered debatable, as it is nowhere specifically granted in the Constitution. In its landmark Marbury versus Madison ruling, the court formalized the power by seizing it.

Presidents have occasionally clashed with the court since then, notably Franklin Roosevelt in 1937. The court had been mowing down his New Deal legislation. He offered a plan to enlarge the number of justices, which would have let him appoint enough to tip the balance of control. (The plan failed.)

In his news conference remarks, President Obama offered two observations.

- The legislative branch of government, in passing the law, and the executive in ratifying it, considered it to be in tune with the Constitution.
- Judges have been known to legislate from the bench, and only another such reach could overturn a law that the president—who is himself a constitutional lawyer—considered to be sound.

On the first point, surely we hope and expect that Congress and the president believe in the validity of the laws they enact. On the second, it is simply a fact that several incumbent Supreme Court justices display an immoderate taste for doctrines of their own choosing.

Nonetheless, down toward Mississippi, Louisiana, and Texas, the 5th Circuit Court of Appeals was peeved by the president's comments. Judge Jerry Smith said he thought the president was challenging the authority of the courts to review acts of Congress. He and two colleagues on the bench ordered the Justice Department to produce a memo explaining what the president said.

Attorney General Eric Holder returned a carefully phrased survey of the long-settled doctrine of judicial review, which the president had not in any way challenged. The memo made no mention of Mr. Obama's remarks, presumably on the assumption that the president does not need judicial permission to have opinions or to express them.

Under the American system, bumptious judges are like relatives. They must be endured.

Bumptious legislators can be another matter, however. Senator McConnell belongs to a faction in Congress that likes to treat the president of the United States with personal contempt.

This is more than coarse arrogance. Speaking to a magazine about Republican priorities for the 2008–2010 Congress, he said, "The single most important thing we want to achieve is for President Obama to be a one-term president." Events have since shown us what he meant. The president's enemies—the word is appropriate—use the nation's legislature to undermine him and confound the wishes of the voters who sent him to the White House.

If we're to speak of officials who cross inappropriate lines, Senator McConnell's example will suffice for me.

VIOLENCE IN SPORTS
APRIL 21, 2012

I once worked with a fellow who was competitive in his marrow. Every transaction included a win/lose quotient. And it wasn't enough for him to win. Someone else had to lose. Someone had to be designated a "loser," and my colleague had to be the agent who applied the tag.

I always thought he missed an important distinction, in the following way.

We like to say that some virtues are conspicuous in the American character. Among these is a determination to persevere against certain circumstances or adversaries. We speak of can-do and never-say-die attitudes.

Of course perseverance would not be considered a virtue if I persevered, say, against a neighbor's objection to my vandalizing his flower beds. Persistence admired is persistence toward a goal that is itself admired. Both the persistence and the goal are perceived to have their own value. If I invent a better mousetrap against all advice that it can't be done, I have produced more than a mousetrap. I have produced an example of attitude and skill.

Attitude and skill are valued in competitive endeavors. Business is one of these. We assume (sometimes naïvely) that competition in business produces better products and services for customers and better value for investors. Success in the competitive world of business is admired when it is presumed to reflect exemplary attitude and skill.

Sports also are competitive endeavors. In sports contests at their proper best, athletes are supposed to test their skill against the rules and circumstances of the game and against the skill of their opponents. They are supposed to test nerve and attitude as well, against fatigue and pressure and surprise adversity—sometimes against bad odds of prevailing against a superior foe. We praise athletes who display "mental toughness"—an unyielding determination to prevail. This is why the cheers are louder when underdogs win.

My former colleague considered himself a sportsman. But for him, in sports as in other endeavors, competition wasn't about excelling. It was merely about defeating others.

The same is broadly true, alas, across sports of all kinds nowadays. An ethic of winning through excellence had been adulterated by an ethic of defeating others through expedient means.

The means run from small to large. Basketball coaches may be noted for their skill at baiting referees. Or whole programs may be corrupt. Recruiting scandals are a fixture in big-time college sports. Academic cheating scandals are, too.

In some sports—football, basketball, hockey, and others—violence is implicit in physical contact. It is supposed to be bounded by rules and by standards of principled behavior. But when the goal is simply to bring an opponent down, boundaries fall and rules bend.

Especially in big-money professional sports, violence may be among the overtly chosen means of winning. Professional basketball includes intentional hard fouls that are meant to intimidate. Hockey teams employ players whose specialty is fighting. Football players cultivate reputations for especially aggressive, punishing play.

All of this brings us to the New Orleans Saints of the National Football League. The Saints have been penalized by the league for running a bounty system in which players received cash rewards for injuring or incapacitating opponents.

That is, Saints players took payoffs for behavior that would be felonious in other settings. The idea was to stack the deck: to deplete the opposing ranks so that the Saints' better players would be pitted against the other team's lesser players. The scheme was about recording the higher score, but it was not about doing a better job with the skills and tactics of football.

Nearly half the players on the Saints' roster took the money. Something more than cheating is at issue here—something more than violating the rules of the NFL business conglomerate. The Saints scandal offends a basic sense of right and wrong. And it's not like a willingness to betray principle suddenly infected these young men when New Orleans hired them. They brought it with them in a concept of competitive sport that could embrace a plan to limit genuine competition.

The Saints' case is an extreme, yes. But it's an extreme of a regrettably familiar notion that winning and achievement are necessarily the same thing.

THE GOP'S HOLY WARS
APRIL 27, 2012

In an old saying: Opinions are like sphincters. Everybody's got one.

This formulation is inelegant but not inconsequential. It cautions us not to be heedlessly fond of our own point of view.

More caution would be useful in the US Congress, where the arrogance of doctrinaire Republicans has produced a perfect storm of governmental incompetence. Louisiana's freshman Rep. Jeff Landry could be their poster boy. He has announced that even if the president is fellow Republican Mitt Romney, the White House has leave to tinker only with the smaller stuff. The big decisions, Landry said, belong to him and his allies. "We're supposed to drive the train."

The Republican holy war against diversity of viewpoint doubly compromises a Congress that has already defaulted on proper obligations. Members of one party slight their duty to serve voters of every party. Ideologues cling to their polar positions and leave the center sparsely populated.

But the center is where the main work of democracy must be done. There, paths forward are found by people who understand that politics are a tool, not a weapon. There, political craftsmen— a dying breed, alas—are willing to do the glamourless, sleeves-up work of tending to the nation's business. They hold this duty above mere partisan advantage.

Congress's default is conspicuous in the Republican-controlled House of Representatives, where Speaker John Boehner's idea of leadership is to sneer at the president of the United States, and Majority Leader Eric Cantor wears his personal ambition like an ugly necktie. While they posture, rookies entertain delusions of giving orders to the White House. As a rule, the American public has little appetite for extremists. Perhaps, over time, the voters will send Congress a larger supply of members who understand the difference between being elected and being anointed.

A loss of political craft also has been conspicuous in the serial disgrace of the Republican presidential primaries. The candidates settled largely for invective and for insinuations that opinions other than their own were not only different but inferior.

We may not be surprised these days when politicians ask us to believe they are made of better stuff. We should be concerned, however, when the politicians themselves begin to believe it. The result, as seen in the Republican primaries, is self-serving noise with nothing coherent to say about appropriate options in public policy. The candidates were not able to parse democracy's language of balanced ends and means, because they had no taste or talent for it.

And there isn't much relief in sight. In settling on Mitt Romney as their nominee, the Republicans are about to choose a bandleader with a tin ear. He was politically clumsy as governor of Massachusetts. As a presidential candidate, he looks stiff and uneasy because he is. Romney is genuinely uncomfortable with the public conversations of presidential politics. He doesn't know how to speak to the electorate.

The atrophy of thought and ability in today's Republican party is sad to see.

THE DEATH PENALTY
MAY 5, 2012

I am opposed to the death penalty. Always have been. Yet I've also been nagged lifelong by the fact that perfectly decent people support it.

Their conscience is good as mine, their moral sense as robust. They feel the death penalty for certain crimes is appropriate—even desirable and necessary.

Some see it as a defensive resource. They note that, as a bulwark against crime, our criminal justice system can seem to be a screen door against the wind. But dangerous felons who've been executed can't be released to do further harm. At least one measure of public safety is thus guaranteed.

Other proponents have in mind a concept of proportionate consequences. The notion is familiar: Let the punishment fit the crime. It would not be right for murder to carry a five-dollar fine, or jaywalking a prison sentence. With laws that define crime and fix penalties, a society details its values. Proponents of the death penalty feel that some offenses are so vile they deserve ultimate punishment. And they feel it's important for society to say so in its statutes.

On the other side of the ledger—my side—the ultimate punishment can be the ultimate mistake. Innocent people can be executed. To avoid this horror, a civilized country should go to every possible length. Our country tries but does not always succeed.

Even where innocents are not involved, capital punishment falls more often on minorities and the poor. Here, the penalty has nothing at all to do with proportionate consequences. It has to do with the socioeconomic status of defendants and vagaries of attitude among prosecutors, judges, and jurors. Within one state or even one city, the same crime can send a white defendant to prison and a black defendant to death row.

But of course these reservations beg the central question: Is it ever right to impose capital punishment? Given a heinous crime and fully established guilt, can the state legitimately put someone to death?

I say no, for reasons that are essentially personal: I do not absolve myself of responsibility by licensing the state to do what I would not do with my own hands.

Thus my disagreement with proponents is over the best location for a moral boundary. The disagreement is fundamental and very likely intractable.

Our system of government is designed to respect and mediate among fundamental disagreements. I have a right to my conscience; you have a right to yours. I may use the vote to assert my views, but my feeling that I'm in the right does not make my vote worth more. Those who cast more votes prevail, and experience suggests that my view on the death penalty will not prevail in my lifetime.

Still, there is room and need for a larger discussion of the criminal justice system, which doesn't reliably work as it should.

Whether it is thought too harsh, too lenient, or simply careless, the system is widely perceived to be capricious. In the aggregate, the perception is valid. Too many facilities are overcrowded and underfunded. Too much court process is driven by a need to settle cases expediently and keep the docket moving.

The system denies the speedy trial promised in the US Constitution. It denies consistent and proportionate punishment. It causes a chronic low fever of public fear that proven offenders are leaked out to do more harm.

Issues of crime and justice in a complex society are themselves complex, of course. Along with symptoms, causes must be considered—notably the causes rooted in socioeconomic desperation. But we should not push causal notions so far as to make them a libel on poor people or let them obscure another important point: timely, certain, and consistent punishment does have a proper societal value.

And on the issue of capital punishment, fewer might favor it if fewer considered it the only sure way to keep dangerous people away from the rest of us.

ROMNEY AND THE RICH
MAY 24, 2012

I got another letter from Uncle Barlow the other day. He writes me sometimes when he's troubled or confused.

I should explain that I'm not sure he's really my uncle. Some in the family say he's Aunt Hettie's love child and not really her baby brother. I guess nobody ever came right out and asked her. She was not the kind of person you questioned.

And I should mention that I'm not sure Barlow is really his name. It could be. Out in the country where he lives, just about every other person is named Barlow. Even the county is named Barlow. So, it could be his name, or it could be a geographic nickname, like Tex or Scotty.

Anyhow, here's what he had to say.

Dear Nephew,

We've got a situation here in Barlow County. Oh, my, do we have a situation. It's not as bad as the time the loading door on the grain elevator gave way and main street got covered with corn. (An avalanche of corn is a sight to see, let me tell you.) But it's a mess.

You see, Millie over at the library has got herself into a big wrangle with her bosses on the library board of directors. She wrote a letter to the *Barlow Clarion* saying that this fellow Mitt Romney was a spoiled rich guy who didn't really understand ordinary people. But half the library board is rich people, and they took offense, and told Millie she should keep her opinions to herself.

Well, Millie is one of the sort who get all stiff-necked if you say boo to them. She said she was entitled to her opinions, and she would speak them if she pleased. And then she commenced to speaking them, oh boy, did she ever.

I must say, it appears to me that Millie may have a point or two on her side when it comes to this fellow Romney. For example, he had one of those secret Swiss bank accounts for a while. Now, I can understand a person wanting to switch banks, now that so many of them are treating their customers like milk cows. The Barlow Bank and Trust wants to charge me a fee for everything except combing my own hair. When I was there the other day I asked them why don't they go ahead and put a turnstile on the door. They acted like their feelings were hurt.

And I can understand that if a fellow manages to put together a little extra money he might want to keep it out of sight, so the in-laws don't get notions. But Switzerland? Millie says there must have been something funny about the money if he wanted to hide it that way. I don't know if I'd go that far, but it sure doesn't look very good, man running for president putting money in a foreign bank. Are they giving away cellphones or something over there when you open a new account?

Also, I read in the *Clarion* that one of Romney's old business partners has written a book saying the super-rich are doing the rest of us a favor by being so well off. They only spend part of their money on themselves, he says, and they invest the rest of it in ways that make new opportunities for everybody else.

I'm not any kind of economist, so I'm sure I can't follow the ins and outs of all that he says in his book. But I do notice that rich folks are apt to live pretty high on the hog, so maybe they're enjoying their money at least a little bit. It seems to me that if some of them were willing to do without quite so many houses, cars and boats, they might be able to spread around even more opportunity.

Anyhow, I'll bet Romney will wish his friend hadn't chosen right now to publish his book, because for little folks like me it sounds mighty selfish and fat-headed. Sort of like the guy doesn't really understand ordinary people.

But I was talking about Millie and the library bunch. Oh, my goodness, what a mess. Millie has a pretty sharp tongue when she gets wound up, and she finally aggravated Orlo Babcock. He owns the tractor dealership out on the bypass. He said she didn't respect the free enterprise system, and maybe he ought to take an extra look at the library's financials to make sure she was running the place like a proper business.

I guess he must have jumped on Millie pretty bad, and that aggravated Floyd from the elevator and Scooter from the cafe. They told Orlo they worked hard for their money, and thought they had a pretty close acquaintance with the real-life side of the free enterprise system, and anyway what the hell did running a business have to do with operating a tax-paid public service ?

Orlo called them free-spending do-gooders. Then the whole board started taking sides. The fight took off from there, and now it's got a life all its own. I think they may even have forgotten what started the whole thing. They fight over the rug lint.

Trouble is, while they're fighting, nothing else gets done. They're getting close to the time when they have to agree on next year's library budget, and if they don't meet the deadline they'll have to shut the place down. Bang! Just close the doors.

That's when I made my mistake. I decided to sit down with Orlo and try to talk some sense. Even though he's pretty much of a big shot now, I've known him since we were in 4-H together and I taught him how to worm a horse.

So I got together with Orlo and just laid it right out plain. I guess maybe I was pretty blunt. I said, Orlo, look here. Y'all are not keeping your obligations. You need to quit fighting and take care of proper business.

He said I didn't understand the principle of the thing. I said, Orlo, the principle of the thing is that you folks are supposed to be doing a job for the public, not strutting your pet notions.

Well, even on his best days, Orlo is the kind of fellow who can strut sitting down. He didn't listen to me, much less try to talk good sense to the others. They have gone right on fighting, and letting their proper business go to the dogs.

Millie says they are acting just like the U.S. Congress, and in Millie's book that's just about the worst thing you can say about a group of people. She says we ought to throw all of them out and vote in a new bunch.

I'm not sure if she was talking about the library bunch or the Congress. Could pretty easy be both, come to think of it.

I hope this letter finds you well, and that things are going smoother up there in the city than they are out here where I live.

Sincerely,

Your Uncle Barlow

MUSIC IN OUR SOULS
JUNE 1, 2012

H is name was new to me, and these many years later I have lost
it from memory. He was a tall man, bowed but not bent. He
wore bib overalls. His long face was weathered. Thinning, salt-and-
pepper hair was slicked straight back. His fingers were knobbed
and gnarled, his few teeth badly stained.

In his rough hands the fiddle looked like something he'd
picked up by mistake. When he appeared, the little pickup band
went silent with something like awe. One of them bent to whis-
per to another. I caught only "...thought he was dead." The tall
man tucked the fiddle under his chin, put the bow to it, and soon
turned every head within earshot. The high, sweet music was pure
as moonlight.

Wordlessly, one by one, the others joined in. The bass player
first, softly, then the guitar, and then the banjo, each finding his
place and staying faithfully in it, so that what they made together

was seamless and perfect—and would be heard, we all knew, only once, in this moment they had conjured out of nothing.

We were in a vast Carolina pasture. It was my first fiddler's convention. My friend and I had gone on a last-minute impulse. Though we would have been horrified to hear it said of us, I think that in some corner of our minds, we were city boys presuming to go and peer at the rubes.

However, I found there a portal to a realm of art and culture that has fascinated me lifelong. From that muddy field, I went on to learn about John and Alan Lomax, folklorists and musicologists who field-recorded thousands of American folk songs for the Library of Congress and hugely affected contemporary music. (The FBI didn't like Alan Lomax's leftist attitudes and subjected him for years to one of their zany snooping enterprises.) I learned about such unlikely pioneers as Huddie Ledbetter, aka Leadbelly, who sang his way out of a Texas prison (pardoned by a governor who enjoyed his stuff) and may have single-handedly saved the twelve-string guitar from fading into disuse and obscurity.

I learned about the songs people used to preserve the heritage they brought to America from all over the world. In some you could hear the skirling of bagpipes, in others the groans of slaves. Some were beautiful, some not. Some of the stories they told were uplifting, some not. But the songs and their stories were true, in the way that a thing is true if it says something right about the work and reward of being human.

I am in mind of all this because of the death of Arthel Lane "Doc" Watson, the North Carolina mountain man who exerted his own transforming influence on American music. He is remembered as a guitar stylist, and that he surely was, changing our very concept of the instrument and its uses. He is remembered as an exemplar of Appalachian roots music, and that he surely was, singing out the dignity and grace of a people subjected elsewhere to rude caricature.

But his music crossed many boundaries of style. In this he was an exemplar of more than lore and technique. In Doc Watson—as in Leadbelly and many others—the inborn genius of the man lay in his being a lens upon the alchemy of music in the human spirit.

We are creatures who gaze at stars and see faces in the clouds. And the music that comes down to us from always and everywhere tells us this one more thing about ourselves: no ghastly grief or trial has ever been able to make us into creatures who imagined to live without husbanding our memories or without singing.

The novelist William Faulkner knew that art is a manifestation of the better parts of us. When he accepted the Nobel Prize for Literature in 1949, he spoke of it this way:

> ...I believe that man will not merely endure; he will prevail. He is immortal, not because he alone among creatures has an inexhaustible voice, but because he has a soul, a spirit capable of compassion and sacrifice and endurance. The poet's, the writer's duty is to write about these things. It is his privilege to help man endure by lifting his heart, by reminding him of the courage and honor and hope and pride and compassion and pity and sacrifice which have been the glory of his past. The poet's voice need not merely be the record of man, it can be one of the props, the pillars to help him endure and prevail.

Music is also the poet's voice, of course. Doc Watson knew that high art in poetry and music may be found in cow pastures as well as concert halls. Thus, when he chose the inscription for a statue erected in his honor, it said: "Just One of the People."

Yes, precisely.

SINFUL LIFESTYLES
JUNE 10, 2012

I got a letter from my Uncle Barlow the other day. He's feeling nervous right now.

It seems the ladies' genealogical society has decided to do a biographical history of Barlow County. They want to interview him. Trouble is, the chronology of his marriage to Aunt Rose and the birth of their son Willie doesn't bear close examination.

He isn't ashamed of it or anything. He loved Aunt Rose dearly until the day she died, and Willie grew up to be a fine man. The problem is, the genealogical society is pretty much the same group as the ladies auxiliary of the First Barlow Church. If they get any idea that a man hasn't been walking the straight and narrow, they send a committee to try to save him. The last time they tried to save Uncle Barlow, he had to hide his jug for three weeks. It made him awfully cranky.

Here's what Uncle Barlow had to say.

Dear Nephew,

I declare, I just don't know what I'm going to do with my television set. On the entertainment shows, the commercials take up as much time as the program. I've tried and tried, but it just aggravates me something awful. So I thought maybe I'd stick to the newscasts, but no matter which one I watch, it feels like they're trying to talk me into something. I mean, can't they just tell me what's happening and leave it at that? (I do figure I understand why those anchor people make a lot of money. I'd hate to think what they must spend on hair spray.)

Anyhow, I decided I'd stick to watching comedians for a while. At least I know they're clowning on purpose. That's how I stumbled across this fellow the other night who was talking about this gay marriage thing that's getting so much attention nowadays. He said he doesn't have any trouble at all understanding why gay marriage should be prevented. He said if we let gay people go around being gay right out in the open, and getting married just like everybody else, pretty soon everybody will want to be gay. Then there won't be any more babies, and the red Chinese will overrun us. He said gay marriage isn't a personal issue, it's a geopolitical threat.

Of course he was funning, but it did get me to thinking about all those man-on-the-street interviews where somebody gets their serious face on and says it's important for the government to declare that marriage has to be between a man and a woman. Now, I don't want to sound like I'm always faulting the TV people, but I just don't understand why these interviewers never ask the obvious question: Why? Why is it important for the government to say that marriage has to be between a man and a woman? Who gets hurt if gay people get married?

Now, it appears to me that a lot of the folks who are anxious about gay marriage are church folks, so I went over to the First Barlow Church to put the question directly to Pastor Throckmorton. I said, Preacher, why should gay people not get married? He said, Because gayness is a sinful lifestyle, and gay people should be cured of wanting to choose it.

Now, that brought me up short. I had always thought of choosing a lifestyle as being sort of like deciding whether you wanted to live in the city or the country. But sex? I remember back in my teens, when Wanda Hightower got to jumping around in that little cheerleader skirt, the thoughts that rushed all over me didn't wait to be chosen. No, sir. They just swarmed up strong all on their own. Many a time I had to keep my coat in my lap for the whole game.

So I asked the preacher if he meant that anybody could be gay. I said, Preacher, could you be gay?

Well, I thought his eyeballs were going to pop right out of his head. He turned all red in the face and got so winded he had to sit down. He commenced to shouting all kinds of no, no, nevers, and I decided it was probably a good time for me just to hush and let him go on.

And I got to thinking that maybe I shouldn't have come there anyway, because I never have had much luck understanding those folks over at the First Barlow Church. They swarm in there on Sundays and talk about loving their neighbors, and then they go around all week acting like they never heard a word of it. I remember once when a couple of the old ladies got the notion that I spent a little too much time with my jug, and darned if they didn't track me down and get all over me about changing my ways. It didn't feel to me like I was being loved. It felt to me like I was being weighed and found wanting.

I guess Preacher Throckmorton and them feel like folks should follow some proper rules in life, and I guess that's OK. But they do seem mighty eager to appoint themselves to choose the rules and do the enforcing. And I have to say, there's just something unkind in that part of it.

That got me to thinking about kindness. And you know who I came up with? Cousin Frank. Actually, I guess, you probably never knew him. He was a lot older. The family used to call him our "confirmed bachelor."

What should I say next about Cousin Frank? Isn't it funny how we decide to go about explaining somebody to somebody else? Well, I guess I've already said the most important thing. He was a kind man. He was a druggist by trade. Owned a little drug store and pharmacy here in town. And he was a helper by nature. Always going a step or two out of his way to give some help to folks he didn't necessarily owe it to.

Some of it was little things. Like, he'd notice if customers weren't refilling their prescriptions on time. And if they didn't, he'd find just the right way to mention it without being nosy. He might lean over to Doc Martin at the Rotary

Club meeting and say something like, I wonder how the Widow Cumbee is doing? She hasn't been in my store in quite a while. Right away the doc would know she wasn't taking her medicine like she ought, and he'd have the nurse call her up.

And some of Cousin Frank's helping was with bigger things. He was always one of the first to volunteer for the Rotary Club service projects. And he'd go over to the home on Sundays just to read to people or chat with them and keep them company. One of them was the Widow Cumbee's mother in law, old Mother Cumbee. She had Alzheimer's. She liked to sit on Sunday afternoons and stare at one particular tree. Well, Frank would go over there and sit and just hold her hand and stare at that tree himself for hours like it was the most beautiful thing in the world.

Anyhow, the particular thing about Cousin Frank was, everybody knew he wasn't partial to women, and nobody cared, because nobody thought it made him less the fine person they knew him to be. He was the best man you would ever want to meet.

That was what was going through my mind while I sat there and waited for the preacher to calm down to a walk. I could see the conversation wasn't going anywhere, and I just thanked him for his time and shook hands to leave. So we never did get around to talking any more about it, and I never got around to asking him why the government should make laws to suit the rules of his church, or how that might work if somebody else's church could round up more votes than his could, and I never did get a common sense answer to that first question: Why?

About the time I got to the door, the preacher shook his finger and warned me that I shouldn't be so cavalier about homosexuality. I had to look up "cavalier" when I got home, but I had already caught the meaning of the way he said it. It was like he wanted me to be afraid in some way.

I thought that was a mighty curious way for a preacher to behave, and so I'm more confused now than I ever was about this whole thing. Maybe the next time you visit here in Barlow County I could introduce you to Pastor Throckmorton, and you could help me understand how he and his folks could be so hostile about something that doesn't hurt them one speck.

But if you ever do meet him, I recommend you don't ask him if it would be possible for him to be gay. He seems to be mighty touchy about any notion of that sort.

Sincerely,

Your Uncle Barlow

HARD-HEARTED RELIGION
JUNE 23, 2012

This time it's Presbyterians. Congregations are breaking away from the Presbyterian Church USA because of its "liberal" drift. They call their preferred alternative a "biblically based" approach to church life. They'll travel their own chosen path.

This time it happens to be Presbyterians, but the story is familiar across Christian denominations. Faith is equated with a particular line of dogma. The dogma becomes a reason to drop the hands of selected fellows. An ethic of rejection prevails.

Schism is not new in the Christian church, and neither are disagreements over biblical authority or is resistance to change—habit being comfortable in human institutions as well as human beings. History is full of such disputes.

Still, events of our own time and place merit attention.

In today's America, discussions of biblical authority are likely to be muddled. Our popular culture is textured by an ersatz scientific skepticism that questions everything but itself, and by epic biblical ignorance. (Exhibit A might be some of the debate about supposed conflict between the Bible and the theories of Charles Darwin. There is no real conflict, but a vernacular quarrel endures nonetheless. Hearsay versions of 150-year-old science are proclaimed as if they were holy writ, and the Bible is freighted with claims it does not make by people who haven't read it.)

The Bible is not a book in our contemporary sense. It is certainly not a history book, as no such thing was known in the years when it was created. It is a conflation of sermons, songs, poems, letters, and narratives written at different times and different places by different people for different audiences, all for different reasons.

The Bible is a collection of human attempts across thousands of years to express an understanding of God. Understandings varied with circumstance. Considered only as an array of separate parts, the Bible is a jumble of inconsistencies and contradictions. Considered as a whole, it tells an evolving story about human experience of the divine.

All of which is to say that the Bible cannot be typified by a single passage or group of passages. Thus citations of Biblical authority may be highly selective. And sure enough, in today's church upheavals, they often are. Common triggers of upset among conservative churchgoers are matters of sex, reproduction, and gender role. They are seized upon as if they were central in Christian scripture. But they are not.

We should be careful about begrudging others their point of view, lest they welcome license to begrudge us ours. The very sweep of the Bible makes it approachable from different directions.

But it is fair to ask what's really happening when people insist they'll stand only on one small corner of its grand tapestry. It is fair to say that selective citations of biblical authority are, in fact, expressions of a point of view. It is reasonable to suspect that cultural bias is being broadcast through the voice of the church and called religion.

Of course every organized church functions at risk of putting words in the mouth of God. A principal admonition of the original Christian message went to that very point. It cautioned against claiming divine mandate for rules of human choosing. In particular, it charged the theocracy of its day with being hard-hearted and legalistic.

In today's denominational wrangles, the conservative church favors words that are exclusionary. The church adopts the posture of a club. Divine welcome is subject to the approval of human insiders. At its most extreme, the Christian right favors words of self-righteous condemnation. The language is...well, hard-hearted and legalistic.

This crabbed and narrow view is nothing like what really is central in Christian scripture: a call to human community and social justice. In the injunction to love one's neighbor, there is no room for any kind of moral caste system.

SETTLING FOR BAFFLEGAB
JULY 8, 2012

Years ago, before the Soviet Union collapsed, a friend of mine worked in Washington for his hometown newspaper. At a diplomatic reception he found himself standing in a corner with a reporter for the official Soviet press. My friend had taken a few extra drinks. Part of their conversation went roughly as follows.

> My friend: C'mon, Yuri, you've been in our country for a couple of years. Surely you have to admit that our system is better than yours.
> Yuri: Noncommittal grunt.
> My friend: You've seen our system up close. We have representative government. People can choose their leaders.
> Yuri: Mildly irritable grunt.
> My friend: C'mon Yuri, how can you possibly say you don't like our system?

Yuri, with a cold glare: If you were honest with yourself about "your system," you would admit that your elected leaders have far more in common with each other than with the people they supposedly represent.

Politicians of every kind have this ethic in common: they are willing to have power over the rest of us, and they are disposed to keep it to themselves and their fellow party members. Thus Yuri would not be surprised by the polarization of today's public affairs. While it rises from cultural and economic tensions that test the public's sense of well-being, it is stoked by an ugly struggle for partisan tenure in the driver's seat.

The partisan ethic elevates the interests of political organizations above the interests of the public. And it creates a vocabulary—an idiom—that adulterates democratic process.

Idiom is useful in private and public conversation. It helps us make certain kinds of points economically. But with overdoses of the partisan ethic, idiom strays into caricature. Politicians on the right are painted as flint-hearted plutocrats who would gladly grind the faces of the poor. Politicians on the left are called addle-pated do-gooders who like to fund their good works with other people's tax money.

These images cross an important line. They invite disregard and distrust. In this way, electoral and public policy decisions come to be styled as good-guy/bad-guy contests: It is not necessary for us to do the work of making informed decisions. We need only give power to the folks in the white hats.

The notion that our nation's options can be so simple is silly on its face. Likewise the notion that this political party or that one has transcended the limits of human nature and can be relied upon, ipso facto, to Do the Right Thing.

The selfish temptations of power touch every ideology. In political parties they excite the institutional instinct for self-perpetuation.

They can carry partisan careerists and true believers to destructive extremes, as in today's behavior by one hot-eyed faction of Congressional Republicans. (Adherents of honorable Republican traditions can only cringe and shelter in the maxim that an idea is not responsible for everyone who claims to believe it.) Playing to one angry segment of the electorate, these toughs commandeer the people's legislature to make their own private war against a duly elected Democratic president. Abetted by a blinkered and inept Republican leadership, they have dragged the Congress of the United States into historic disrepute.

Extremists do not last in American public life. In due time, those now plaguing Congress will be curbed or replaced. Of greater concern for the long term is a chronic, cliché-driven inattention to the realities of our national affairs.

Partisans on the right inveigh against big, expensive, intrusive government. And wariness on this score is warranted.

But the favorite clichés of the right do not acknowledge that truly limited government is long gone. It would no longer be sufficient. The task of running this country is too complex. The dangers afoot in the world are too great. American government is big, and it's going to stay big no matter who's in charge—witness the record of several Republican presidents who rank high among modern architects of huge government enterprise. The enduring question for our country is not whether government should be big or small. The question is, to what uses should big government be put?

In this connection, partisans on the left call upon us to do a better job with social equity. And well they should. The inequities that persist even yet in this prosperous country are not morally or politically tenable.

But the favorite clichés of the left do not forthrightly own one of their necessary methods: empowering government to take something that belongs to you and give it to me. Neither do they remind us that this power, once given, remains in place to be used in the discretion of the unknowns who will one day succeed the incumbents of the moment. Neither do they squarely face the truth of charges that government programs are inherently vulnerable to waste and corruption.

With rhetoric that advertises false choices and disguises real ones, politicians invite charges of cynicism. Clearly, some of them are guilty. They treat politics entirely as a game of appearances. They aim to succeed by glad-handing the electorate and tricking up new costumes for a single message: Trust me. You can't trust the others, but you can trust me.

If we rest with charges of cynicism, however, we merely join those who traffic in simplistic formulations. A conspiracy theory won't do. Not all politicians are cynical.. Other factors combine to fill our national affairs with partisan sloganeering—language that is not meant to illuminate choices but only to persuade voters to take sides.

One factor is public indifference. Most people don't regularly vote. Among those who do, not a few vote out of ignorance or prejudice. Earnest politicians who might want to get beyond slogans face a huge obstacle: At any given moment, most of the electorate isn't listening.

I can't render public service if I can't get elected. I can't get elected if I can't get you to vote for the ideas I represent. I can't get you to vote for me if I can't get your attention. And to get your attention in today's America, I need the vivid phrase, the colorful image, the sound bite, and the photo op. Nothing else reliably works. A sorry expedient becomes the norm.

The special tensions of the moment are circumstantial: an historic economic swoon; sea changes in the demographics of the population; the newly inescapable closeness of the world community.

These circumstances, and our experience of them, will settle. The chronic failure of better conversation about our national priorities is a deeper thing, and worrisome.

LIFTED PINKIES
JULY 16, 2012

The good news is, we discuss public art in my town.

That's also the bad news.

My town is a pretty place, by and large. The streets are clean, the shoulders mowed and trimmed. Plentiful parks are well kept. A widespread tree canopy is valued in civic tradition and protected by local ordinance.

In towns as in people, an essential regard for appearance is a virtue. You and I may differ on particulars. Our standards of fashion, decor, and maintenance may not match. But below a certain threshold, a slob is a slob, an eyesore is an eyesore, and a dump is a dump.

With an eye toward maintaining a pleasant community aspect, the government of my town uses a fraction of its tax income to purchase works of art for display in public places. These objects are placed on major street corners, in parks, and in the medians of boulevards. One interesting set is spread along the right-of-way of a commuter rail line.

Opinions of these selections are, of course, not unanimous. In my own view, some of them are fine indeed, and some look like the runner-up entries in a grammar-school craft contest. Eye of the beholder and all that. Overall, they are a valid investment of public money. They are a nice dash of seasoning in the quality of life hereabouts.

From time to time, new purchases are announced. On these occasions, some taxpayers object to the selections with extra vigor. Then, trouble begins. Then, the culture mavens emerge from their salons to scold the common folk. (In the squall of condescending clichés, one perennial and mystifying favorite is an assertion that "good" art should "provoke." This standard does not distinguish, for me, an experience of good art from an experience of interstate gridlock.)

Let us leave to its perpetrators the odd notion that taxpayers should not have—or at least should not express—opinions about the uses made of their money. Consider instead the proposition that taste is the province of the refined few, who will let the rest of us know what should be admired.

Taste prescribed by others is not taste at all but only conformity. We are allowed to have independent tastes, and in fact we do. They may be refined by experience or education, but they are instilled by neither. Our tastes are part of us.

We all can cite examples that refute elitist stereotypes. Mine include a waterfront laborer whose knowledge and grasp of opera were stunning. One of my favorite paintings was done by an inmate of San Quentin's death row. A Midwestern undertaker wrote a book of essays in some of the most graceful prose I have ever read. (*The Undertaking: Life Studies from the Dismal Trade*, by Thomas Lynch.)

Such examples hint at something essential in us. We are makers and partakers of patterns and images, of poems and songs, of narratives that seek to explain the way things happen and the way things are. We want to apply from within ourselves some suggestion of order and sense to our existence. We feel that we should, we feel that we can, and, from the first time an image of a stag was painted on the wall of a cave, we have always tried.

Others bring to this idea far more than anecdotal evidence. Anglican theologian N. T. Wright is one. In the first pages of his multivolume look at the concept of God as perceived through the Christian New Testament, he makes an interesting choice of foundation stones to lay down before his readers. He does not begin with theological concepts. He begins with a detailed explication of the nature of storytelling: "Stories are one of the most basic modes of human life…Stories…provide a vital framework for experiencing the world."

On this point Bishop Wright's outlook was shared by American drama critic Walter Kerr. His 1962 book *The Decline of Pleasure* argued that the fine arts had been consigned to second-class citizenship in modern American culture. This he lamented as a fundamental loss. He said that music and art and literature emerge from—and therefore speak to—our human nature. If we diminish our regard for them, he said, we permit a part of ourselves to wither.

In this view, Kerr wrote, the highest tastes can never be the province of the few. They are inborn and personal: "For taste is either personal (yours, mine, Henry's) or it does not exist. There is no chemical element in the universe that invariably produces it in a certain solution…Taste is never a law. It is always an entirely private love."

So, for my own part, I will go on being glad that the leaders of my town buy us a little adornment from time to time. I will go on hoping they buy more of what I like and less of what I don't. I will cling to the view that beauty belongs to everyone and that wonderful gems may be cut and polished for us by the ordinary people next door, to wit: a passage from Kerr's book that he attributes to an unnamed columnist in an unnamed, small-town American newspaper:

> Saw three birds abreast, wheeling leisurely in great circles, the movements of six wings synchronized and perfect...as they momentarily held the morning sun and then winged away into the distance. Had I been an ornithologist, I would have identified these creatures on the wing by name, delved into their family tree, and explained something of their habits. Seeing them in the eyes of a weather prophet, I might have announced them as omens of fair weather or of rain and related stories of the past that would prove my predictions. As a philosopher perhaps I would see them as symbols of peace and harmony and would expound at length the examples that nature has set for mankind. Being none of these, I saw them only as three white birds in a morning sun and thought them beautiful.

I REMEMBER A MOUNTAIN MAN
JULY 21, 2012

Don't it always seem to go
That you don't know what you've got
'Til it's gone
They paved paradise
And put up a parking lot

"Big Yellow Taxi"
Joni Mitchell, 1970

He is long dead now, but he still deserves his privacy, so I'll call him Mr. Smith. He was a weathered old mountain man from deep in the coves and hollows of western North Carolina.

He and his wife lived a few miles down a dirt track carved into steep hillsides. At one edge of it, rock faces jumped up so close you could touch them without stretching in your seat. At the other edge, the land dropped sharply to a river bottom far below. The little road was not wide enough for two cars to pass. Shallow turn-outs had been scooped out of the hills here and there. If two driv-ers met, one backed up to the nearest turnout to let the other by.

You walked the last fifty yards or so to the Smiths' place. The slope up to their dooryard was too steep to drive. Their little cin-der-block house was tucked against a second slope. Around it, the walls of a small valley swept up and out. I once asked him how much of it they owned. He said everything I could see had been in his family for generations. He called it "my mountain."

Mr. Smith was in his eighties when I knew him, born and reared almost all the way to manhood in the late nineteenth century. He knew all the old mountain ways and still kept many. He knew how to make a toothbrush from a sugarbush branch and a broom from nothing more than a hardwood tree limb. I suspected that Mr. Smith knew how to make a little liquor, too, but he never said, and I never asked.

He had piped a cold mountain spring through the rear wall of his house. It pooled in a broad concrete basin and then flowed out to a creek that bubbled through his front yard. Jars of food stood in the basin, which served as their refrigerator.

The best spot for a barn was split by that creek. Mr. Smith had felled tree trunks across it and built the barn upon them, strad-dling the stream.

During his working years, he had farmed the flatter parts of his land. In old age he turned to building houses now and then. That was how I met him. He was putting up a vacation house for a friend of mine. He'd designed it, in pencil, on a shirt cardboard that he carried in the bib of his overalls. He built it with only the help of an eighteen-year-old lad who ferried him to the site and did the heavy lifting.

It was a complete, three-bedroom job with a barn-style, gam-brel roof (Mr. Smith called it a "roundin' rafters" roof). On one end were two floors of living quarters. On the other was a great room open all the way to the roof line. Much of the end wall was covered by a stone fireplace with a massive wooden beam for a mantel. Mr. Smith had fashioned the beam from wood on his land. He had built the fireplace himself from field stone that also came from his land.

I was never sure how well Mr. Smith could read or write. But his gifts with stone and wood were remarkable. He added to my friend's house touches we could never have imagined. The door-latching mechanisms were handmade of wood in the old-fashioned way. They worked as well as any you could buy. The gutters and downspouts were of wood in the old way, too. And to carry water away from the foundation, he made spillways from slabs of wild stone. Nature could have placed them herself.

In time, I asked Mr. Smith to build a little cottage for me. My friend had recommended me. You had to be recommended to Mr. Smith.

And my friend advised me: "The mountain people have their own way about some things. They take pride in doing a proper job of what they're paid to do. But their attitude is that they are working with you, not for you. At some point Mr. Smith will make it clear, with words or some kind of gesture, that this is his view. It will be important for you to respond."

I asked, "How will I know when that is happening?"

My friend said, "You'll know. If you pay attention, you'll know."

Sure enough, one very early morning, Mr. Smith roused me with an insistent knock. He said, "I need your help with this ladder."

Still in my pajamas, I helped him carry a ladder down the lane from my unfinished place to my friend's. When we put the ladder down, Mr. Smith looked me in the eye for a conspicuous extra beat and said, "Thank you. I'm grateful for your help."

I paid him by the hour. (He kept track on the back side of that shirt cardboard in his bib overalls.) And I began to sense that he spent more time at my site than I was paying him for. When I asked about it, I discovered that he didn't charge me when rain stopped him from working. But neither did he go home. If he thought the rain wouldn't last, he and the helper sat in the cab of their truck, sometimes for hours, waiting to get a little more done before they left for the day.

I asked him to let me pay at least a little something for his hours on my site, even if he wasn't able to work the whole time. He wouldn't hear of it.

When I go to the mountains nowadays, I think of Mr. Smith. I think of that morning of the ladder, when he and I silently agreed that I had bought his time but not him. I think of his refusal to accept pay for idle time, and of learning to understand that the refusal was for his own sake and not for mine. I remember his knowing how to get a living from hard land and how to make from a length of wood or a mute rock something that did a job and pleased the eye, too. I remember the smile in his eyes when he looked up the slopes of "his mountain" and the warmth in his voice when he described remote spots where the rhododendron blooms were just right and the mountain laurel covered whole hillsides.

When I go to the mountains nowadays, I think of all the craft of life that was in Mr. Smith and is now gone. I'm reminded of what we're covering over with our golf courses and theme parks and bars and boutiques. We are covering not just a landscape but a culture.

We who were privileged to glimpse it should erect markers. We should declare: Something else was here before. Something worthwhile. Something that mattered.

I hope this counts a little in that direction.

US AGAINST THEM
AUGUST 9, 2012

Good-bye to my Juan, good-bye Rosalita,
Adios mis amigos, Jesus y Maria;
You won't have your names when you
ride the big airplane,
All they will call you will be, "deportee"

From "Deportee (Plane Wreck at Los Gatos)"
By Woody Guthrie and Martin Hoffman

During World War II, Congress authorized a program to bring Mexican farm workers into the United States to fill labor shortages caused by the war. Private contractors were to provide transportation to and from the Mexican border. If contractors defaulted, the US Immigration Service filled in.

In 1948, a plane carrying Mexican laborers crashed in Los Gatos Canyon, California. All aboard were killed. Newspaper and radio accounts of the crash named the flight crew but not the twenty-eight Mexican passengers. They were called only "deportees." They were buried in a mass grave. Only twelve were ever identified.

Folk singer Woody Guthrie wrote a poem containing the words above. Later a schoolteacher named Martin Hoffman set it to music. The song became a staple of the American folk music movement in the 1960s.

Guthrie was assailing the cultural bias manifest in the episode: The dead passengers were only hired help. And they were not even from our country. They were not like "us." In death as in life, they mattered less.

Biases are part of being human. Everyone harbors them. We carry around in our heads a kind of personal caste system. We label people: this one is diligent; that one is lazy; the other is greedy. Some lifestyles are wholesome; of others we disapprove. Some vocations are lofty, some menial. On the ladder in our minds, not everyone stands on the same rung.

Our varying views have a common denominator: Some people and their attitudes are essentially like me and mine. But others are essentially different. Those differences mark the border of unfamiliar territory. There, my norms may not be observed; my interests may not be wholly valued. People who are different put me on alert.

Add the catalyst of ethnicity, and our attitudes can reach punitive extremes. The American story is full of examples. When they reached our shores, Italians, Irish, Poles, Dutch, Chinese, and more had to endure disdain, ridicule, abuse, and worse. To this day, African Americans pay a heavy price simply for being who they are.

Newcomers. Outsiders. People who don't look or speak or dress or worship or celebrate or grieve the way we do. They all put us on alert.

The death of those wartime workers marks an example that has exploded anew in the debate of illegal immigration. The debate can be especially heated, even venomous, because it takes place in a powerful new context. Demographic trends are literally changing the nation's face. In about forty years, people who've traditionally thought of themselves the typical American—that is, whites—will be a minority. The surge from south of the border is not just a legal, political, or economic problem. It's a reminder that the way we live together in our own country is headed for fundamental and inescapable change.

Ethnicity also is playing a new role in presidential politics. An election that pits a moderately conservative Republican against a moderately liberal Democrat is complicated by the fact that the Republican challenger, Mitt Romney, is a moneyed patrician, and the Democratic president is African American. Us-versus-them imagery is especially tempting, and some have succumbed. A vivid example comes from former New Hampshire Governor and White House Chief of Staff John Sununu. He declared not long ago that President Barack Obama needs to "learn how to be an American." This would be an exceedingly odd thing to say of a fifth-generation WASP. It resonates—in some ears—because the president is a black man with an unusual name.

(For the sake of a smile, let us note that Sununu was born in Cuba, and his immediate heritage is Palestinian and Greek.)

Unless we find a way to transcend human nature, ethnic tensions are inevitable in a country as diverse as ours. But nowadays they've been heightened by the sheer size of the illegal migration from the south. And other pressures—economic and cultural—have joined to put ugly edges on our national conversation.

Failures of leadership complete the mix. A bankruptcy of ideas has opened politics on the right to proprietorship by second-stringers, ideologues, snake-oil salesmen, and quacks. Republicans themselves acknowledge that their presidential nominee is merely the strongest of a weak bunch.

On all sides we find a contagious portrayal of political notions as moral precepts. In the sadly ironic result, we lose the moral discipline to respect others' points of view. Policy debate becomes a kind of holy war. Candidates are not merely opposed; they are reviled. Public discourse becomes genuinely hostile to differences of opinion.

American democracy should aspire to more than an ethic of intolerance.

THE ROMNEY SANDWICH
AUGUST 23, 2012

I got a letter from Uncle Barlow the other day. Life is getting lively way out there in Barlow County. And he's been watching the national news again, which often stirs him up. Here's what he had to say.

Dear Nephew,

I guess it's been a while since I wrote you. I've been mighty busy. You might remember that the Ladies' Genealogical Society is working on a biographical history of Barlow County. Well, they discovered that my Daddy bootlegged a little whiskey from time to time, and that I drove deliveries for him when I was a young buck. And the trouble is, the Genealogical Society is pretty much the same bunch as the Ladies Auxiliary of the First Barlow Church. When they found out about the whiskey, they took a fit.

Out of the blue I had a flock of them on my porch singing "Come Ye Sinners," and "There Is A Fountain Filled With Blood." The Widow Cumbee was standing over to one side shouting at me to repent, and I want to tell you, when the Widow Cumbee gets wound up she can howl the chrome off a truck bumper. All the commotion scared the tar out of my coon dog Buster, and he got stuck trying to hide under the sofa, and I guess I said some things to the old biddies that I shouldn't have said. So, then I had to go around to each of them and apologize, but every visit had to include another sermon about the evils of whiskey, and that wound up taking quite a while, and that's why I have been mighty busy.

Now, all that hellfire and brimstone put me in mind of catching up on the presidential election, since both the fellows running say the country will go straight to hell if the other one wins. And darned if that thing hasn't started to look like one of those mud-wrestling contests you can see on TV. Matter of fact, someone might want to caution those two fellows about winding up like those wrestlers. I mean, after a while, if they've heaped enough mud on each other, it gets kind of hard to tell which one is which.

Anyhow, I am particularly interested in this fellow Romney, since he is the new one into this presidential business. And I've tried, nephew, honest I've tried. But I just can't figure out what kind of man is walking around inside that fellow's clothes.

I see that while I was busy getting rescued from the jaws of hell, he went overseas to visit a bit. And I guess it took him a little while to get his bearings, seeing as how he started out by saying that the British couldn't organize a fire drill and those Palestinian folks were dumber than a box of hammers. I mean, he probably really does understand that guests shouldn't talk that way.

But the thing that puzzled me was that when he finally did get to what he said was the point of things, which was foreign policy, he just said he had some ideas but he would get around to explaining most of them some other time. I said to Millie over at the library, if that was all he had to say he could have saved airfare and sent them a post- card. Millie said he was never really interested in saying much of anything at all, that he just wanted to have some pictures taken with foreign leaders so he could look presidential.

I should warn you that Millie would just as soon kiss a snake as speak well of a Republican. She says they are just too darned nosy about what women do in their personal lives. She says they would favor chastity belts if they could get away with it. Millie has a mighty sharp tongue about some things, but I do have to say that on matters of sex and birth control and such, this Ryan fellow who is Romney's new sidekick does sound like one of those people who want the government make all of us join their church.

Anyhow, it seems like every other time Romney speaks up, all he wants to say is that President Obama is lower than a suck-egg dog. Now, I guess most of us have already figured out that Romney doesn't think Obama is the man for the job, or else he wouldn't be going to so much trouble to try to get him thrown out. And I guess it's understandable that Romney might get a little hot under the collar about it now and then.

But Millie says (I had to write this down, as Millie has a lot more words than I do) "Personal derision of Barack Obama does not amount to a philosophy of government." For my own self, I would just say that if Romney is elected, he's going to have to do a lot more than cuss Obama to get us through the next four years.

I'd like to know some more about how he might go about that. And here's where I start scratching my head. Darned if he doesn't act like he wants to avoid the whole subject. He says he's got a plan to cut taxes and balance the budget, but he doesn't explain how it would work. He says he's got a plan to lower unemployment, but he doesn't explain how that would work, either. He says he wants to eliminate some federal government office and agencies, but he won't say which ones.

And at the top of the list of things he's mum about, I guess you would have to put his income tax returns. Now, I don't suppose they would show he's done anything illegal. Those tax boys over at the IRS would have been after him long ago for something like that. I just think the returns would show he put a high life priority on getting rich, since you don't get to be as rich as he is by falling off a log. No, sir. (Millie grumbles about him being a rich guy, but I told her that if we didn't allow rich guys to be president we would have eliminated quite a few good ones.)

No, the thing that interests me about this tax return business is that he gets so sniffy when the subject comes up. He acts kind of like you're burping at the dinner table if you even ask. It's almost like he's looking down his nose at the public, which is a strange kind of behavior for someone who wants a lot of folks to vote for him. Matter of fact, this whole business of asking us to choose his plans without really knowing what they are is strange behavior.

Millie says Scooter over at the café is missing a good bet with that mystery meat he serves. She says he should put it on bread and call it a Romney Sandwich.

That Millie. She has a mighty sharp tongue about some things.

I hope you are well. I will try not to let it be so long before I write you again.

Sincerely,

Your Uncle Barlow

WHOPPERS, BEDFELLOWS, AND THE STATE OF THE NATION
SEPTEMBER 7, 2012

I got a letter from my Uncle Barlow the other day. At least I think he's my uncle in some distant way. I've never been completely clear on that. Every time I ask the people in my family who are old enough to know, they just chuckle or change the subject. He's a pretty good old gentleman, though, and he's fond of me, so he writes now and then to discuss what he calls the passing parade of life. He has a particular kind of view of it from his home way out there in Barlow County.

Here's what he had to say:

Dear Nephew,

Well, things are pretty slow hereabouts, if you don't count the fact that Scooter over at the cafe is in trouble again with

From Obama To Trump

his wife Ida. She's been after him to take her up to the city to hear the symphony. Well, Scooter told Floyd over at the grain elevator and hardware store that he would just about as soon listen to a bull farting through a bugle. Trouble was, Scooter didn't know that Ida was in the next aisle shopping for canning jars. She heard every word.

That was when Scooter made his second mistake. He told Ida he was just making a little joke. Now, Ida is mighty fond of her point of view. If she's real serious about something, she wants you to be, too, and she's ready to explain why. She jumped all over Scooter in the worst way. Been giving him down the country for more than a week. He's going around town looking droopy as a wet dog.

I got to thinking that Ida is a little like some of these politicians we've got going around nowadays. I mean the ones that want all of us to have personal opinions just like theirs, and who want laws to make it look like we did even if we don't. There was a bunch of that sort flocked together at that Republican National Convention down in Florida. You'd have thought some of them were handing down heavenly pronouncements, except for the fact that a fair amount of what they had to say wasn't really true.

I guess the hands-down leader in that department was this fellow Ryan who wants to be vice-president. Millie over at the library says he's the kind of politician who would cut down a redwood tree and stand on the stump to make a speech about conservation. You'd think he'd be pretty good with the whoppers by now, seeing as how he's been telling them in a pretty regular way for several years. But darned if he didn't tell one interviewer that he had run one of those

87

marathon races a whole lot faster than he actually did. It's a little thing, I guess, but it's mighty odd. I mean, if you were setting out to lie in public, why would you choose a thing where other people were timing with stopwatches and writing down results? Millie says Ryan acts like he's got liver-mush for brains.

Well, then, along came the Democrats with their own show, and I felt like I ought to watch it, too. They sure did put on a humdinger. I guess maybe a little more of what they said was actually true, although to make proper sense of some of the numbers they were throwing around, you kind of had to close one eye and squint at them sideways. I have never understood why politicians need to get into tall tales when they want to criticize each other. The truth is usually bad enough.

I noticed some movie actors hanging around both the conventions. And I guess that makes a certain kind of sense, seeing as how politicians and actors are in similar lines of work. But it can sure make for some strange sets of bedfellows. When the Republicans chose an actor they wanted to put up at the podium, they went with that Eastwood gent who got his big break making cut-rate Westerns in Spain. I thought Republicans were touchy about that whole outsourcing business, but maybe not so much.

I favor the Democrat bunch this year. I have pretty much decided that. They don't remind me of the Peabodys like the Republicans do.

When I was a boy, the Peabodys lived in a big house on the swell side of town. If the Peabody boys didn't want to be completely alone, they had to hang around with the rest of us from time to time. (Although they would never let girls into their tree house.) But they always acted like they were doing us a favor with their company. Every now and then you would catch one of them looking at you like you had cow flop on your shoes.

And none of the parents liked to go out to eat with old man Peabody. He always found a way to wiggle out of helping with the tip. He kind of acted like it was everybody else's obligation to help him hang onto as much money as he could.

The Peabodys were big churchgoers, which I guess is a fine thing for people to do if they want to. But the Peabodys acted like their church was the only proper one, and they could be mighty pushy about it. One time they tried to get the county board to pass a law closing the Bijou movie theater on Sunday, because their church didn't favor what they called worldly entertainment on the Sabbath. Well, then old Ben Levine said if they were going to start passing Sabbath laws he might have some different notions to offer, and the whole thing got bogged down and finally just went away.

My daddy didn't like the Peabodys one bit, but mostly I just felt sorry for them. They always seemed to be real troubled that everybody in Barlow County didn't think just the same way they did.

I have to go now. I'm going to drop over to the café and see if I can't cheer Scooter up a little bit. His cooking goes straight to the dogs when he's on the outs with Ida, and some folks are starting to talk about taking their lunch trade to the Burger Boy out on the bypass.

I promise to write again real soon.

Sincerely,

Your Uncle Barlow

WHICH SIDE ARE YOU ON?
SEPTEMBER 15, 2012

A s we watch singers and actors taking sides in the presidential election, we may wonder what connects art and politics.

I am not here thinking of the art that has always paid attention to certain kinds of public affairs—songs of protest, for example, or novels that treat social injustice. Rather I have in mind entertainers who trade on their celebrity to magnify mere partisan allegiance.

This is not a major matter. Just a straw in the wind. But straws do show which way the wind is blowing. Celebrity feeds and is fed by popular culture. Celebrity politics suggest an assumption that side-taking is safely consistent with cultural norms. And indeed it is. In America nowadays, the question in the air is not "How can we best live together?" but "Which side are you on?"

The skirmish lines of our culture war often run through religious territory. At one extreme, a faction of Christian conservatives pushes the rest of us to accept a dog's breakfast of religious doctrine and bully-boy politics. Their ardor for religious values includes an ironic disrespect for religious values—other people's, that is. Failing by moral persuasion to induce other people to abandon their values, these self-appointed Christian soldiers resort to force. They want the government to mandate their chosen interpretation of Christian scripture through civil law. This is, of course, dangerous both to religion and to a principled rule of law.

An attitude at the other extreme is not so sharply focused or militant. But it is consequential. It rises from a muddled extrapolation on principles of church/state separation. The concept of freedom of religion has morphed into a cultural expectation of freedom *from* religion. A lot of us feel we have a right to live beyond sight or sound of any manifestation of faith.

The attitude reaches far beyond issues of nativity scenes on courthouse lawns. It reaches into private spheres. Ask a person of faith what kinds of looks may be directed at a murmur of prayer over a restaurant meal. Or consider common social etiquette: Tell an off-color story at a dinner party, and you may be judged merely daring or naughty. But venture a serious consideration of God, and you may be charged with a truly significant breach of manners.

And consider again the weathervane of celebrity. Our popular culture is so ripe for antireligious attitudes that to the pantheon of celebrity liberals and celebrity conservatives, we have now added celebrity atheists.

On either side of the religious skirmish line, groups of us scorn other people's beliefs. On either side of political skirmish lines, groups of us disdain questions of balancing ends and means.

The US Congress will suffice as exhibit A. Once known as the world's greatest deliberative body, it has lost capacity for true deliberation because it has lost respect for the very idea. Moderates are seen as weaklings and treated accordingly. Compromise is equated with failure. Congress wars over trifles and trifles with fundamentals. The nation's business is conducted with the dignity of a soccer riot. The default on sworn duty is especially sharp in the House of Representatives, where a Republican faction is so besotted with ideology that it values nothing else.

All of which brings us back to the weathervane of the presidential election. Here there is no real contest of ideas, not much at all beyond gestures of contempt. Both sides have favored epithet over substance. The Republican ticket has adulterated even this sorry mix with a campaign of audacious falsehood.

And if disdain for the truth is shoddy, Republican strategy contains another element that is downright alarming. The Romney/Ryan ticket plainly intends to reveal as little as possible about specifics of the policies they would take to Washington.

Only two readings are possible here:

- The Republican candidates believe the American people have no right to know what they can expect from their government.
- The candidates know the people have that right but mean to scorn it in hopes of gliding to election on glossy platitudes. They mean to gain the White House by tricking the electorate.

The tenor of this campaign is a spectacular disgrace. We must hope that we are not soon again asked to endure the like of it.

But the campaign is in part the work of party strategists and their hired-gun consultants. Something else is at work in the tenor of our larger national discourse. There, the much-lamented failure of civility is only a symptom. The root failure is one of tolerance. We are surrendering to a notion that different values are illegitimate by virtue of being different.

This is civic laziness. Or perhaps it is only civic weariness. Hard times take a toll.

THE DIVINE PEST
OCTOBER 12, 2012

For no particular reason, these ideas are on my mind lately. Few are original with me, but I like them anyway.

I have several friends who are atheists. They are thoughtful people and good human beings. They care about fundamentals of right and wrong. They are serious about principled behavior.

But as I like to tease them—and I do like to tease them—their creed is not above the contortions, contradictions, and logical embarrassments that afflict other forms of belief.

For starters, if we define atheism as an affirmative rejection of the existence of God, then atheism is ironically focused on the concept of deity. God is, so to speak, fiendishly hard to avoid.

And moving on: Without God, atheism would be an entirely man-made thing. In that respect, if we reason strictly, it would not be wildly different from organizing one's value system around a totem pole or a stone figurine. On the other hand, if there is a

God, then our capacity to conceive of atheism is God-given. The Old Pest has his own taste for irony.

When my atheist friends tease me—and they do like to tease me—they quite accurately point out that similar comments could be aimed in my direction. I am a Christian. (But not today's right-wing kind. I am not under the impression that my political opinions are divinely inspired.)

As an entirely man-made thing, the Christian story would not be a very clever job. The several versions of it don't always jibe. If I'm going to put faith in a tale, my atheist friends tell me, I should search for one whose authors have not left so many seams showing.

If, on the other hand, the Christian God is really up there and watching, God tolerates in events and behavior a good deal that God is said to abhor. As value systems, theism and Christianity are not reliably systematic.

My atheist friends do not persuade me. Neither do I persuade them, if only because I don't try. I never proselytize.

For me, it would be a messy undertaking. The necessary disclaimers alone would leave time for little else. One does not want to be confused with the quacks and slickers who will save your soul for only a modest donation. Neither am I in tune with the churches whose God wants them to build a larger gymnasium.

And I respect the view that religious faith is a private and personal thing usually better left to private and personal resolution. For all these reasons, I long ago concluded that God could soldier on without my help in recruiting.

Thus I do not advertise my faith. Neither do I go to lengths to hide it. The G-word occasionally slips out of me. In our aggressively secular culture, reactions are an interesting study. From friends and family, I usually get loving forbearance. Double-takes from others hint that I might as well have claimed aliens put transmitters in my molars.

But some people take the G-word as a cue for engagement, even though I never mean to use it in that way. Often I find these people are looking for a reality check on honest doubts. We've all had them, if we are awake and alert.

There are so many faiths, they say, and so many varieties of outlook even within a given faith. How can you reconcile a belief in one God with this crazy quilt?

(In what follows I have no aim to persuade, only to avoid the vanity of embroidering my views with phony reservations.)

The proposition does not trouble me. I see no reason why God should not choose to speak to different people in different ways. I am less interested in the differences than in the single thread that runs through them all: belief in a higher order. Societies worldwide include faith-based value systems.

And so the religious impulse is—whatever else—not an artifact of secular culture. It is everywhere, in cultures as different from each other as Earth from Mars. It appears to be inborn. Hence we can usefully wonder: how could it happen, in a Godless universe, that people of all kinds would be born with religious sensibilities?

OK, my doubting questioners say, but what about your Christianity? What about history's litany of ghastly cruelties perpetrated for—and by—the church? What about the outright charlatans through the ages, from dissolute popes to television bunco artists? How do you reconcile the Christian message with all that?

Well, I don't. The first question to ask about the Christian story is not whether it can be claimed by fools and scoundrels. The first question to ask—to belly up and face—is this one: is it true? The central assertion of Jesus' death and resurrection: is it true?

For purposes of argument, I will rule out equivocation. A duly informed answer is possible. For many years my answer has been, "Yes, the story is true. Those things actually did happen."

Here, we moderns reflexively think, *Show me. Prove it, or at least give me good evidence.*

If we simply must indulge the notion of measuring infinity with finite concepts, we may consider history. We know as much about the historicity of Jesus as about other ancient figures whose stories we accept.

Also science (I like this one; my schooling is in mathematics): The pure scientific odds against a chance emergence of earthly life are astronomical.

But in the end there is no Open Sesame, no Rosetta Stone. We will be handed no lens through which, with only a look, we could at last clearly see divine footprints. If we confront it forthrightly, the mystery of faith requires of us what it has required of everyone in human history: we must strive for our own discernment.

From my work at that, the simplest formulation I can offer is the punch line from an old and often-quoted story: I find it easier to believe in God than to believe that our capacities for love and beauty are produced by the molecular chemistry of meat.

In my experience, people who can't bring themselves to embrace religion balk at hierarchical silliness, power-mongering, and greed in religious institutions; or by other forms of rampant hypocrisy among the so-called faithful; or simply by the random cruelty of nature.

Heaven knows—to choose a phrase—they see clearly. But, just as organized religion does not create God, attitudes of unbelief cannot erase God or neutralize grace. In fact, I wonder if the Almighty gets a wry smile out of seeing that antipathy toward religion is so often a product of scrupulous conscience.

NOW THAT IT'S OVER
NOVEMBER 8, 2012

My Democratic friends are glowing with relief this week. They feared Mitt Romney would be elected and impose a dark, conservative vision on the country. I thought their fear was slightly off the mark. Mine was that Romney would prove incompetent to lead the country in any direction.

He tried, in effect, to lie his way into the White House. Had he succeeded, he would have arrived with very little credibility and a conspicuous lack of essential skill. His repeated gaffes in the campaign were not mere slips of the lip. They were the blunders of a man without a grasp of public leadership.

Our system gives us means to curb a president who offers to go to extremes. It does not equip us to endow a president with abilities he simply doesn't have.

———

Lewis Carroll's White Queen would have been untroubled by Romney's shape-shifting candidacy. She boasted that she could believe "six impossible things before breakfast." Those of us who can't may yearn to see through the smoke screen at last and discern what the country has escaped or gained by re-electing Barack Obama.

One of my guesses is that we have gained a higher quality of appointments to the federal judiciary.

The process of judicial appointment has fallen toward a low state as the country has become progressively more comfortable, alas, in viewing the courts as surrogate legislatures. Candidates for the bench are assessed in the kind of terms once reserved for elective office—terms that jurists of an earlier era would rightly have found insulting.

If one were to choose a sports analogy (and I ask forgiveness for doing so), it would be something like this: We no longer mind the notion that the referees may throw the game. We have settled for wanting referees who will throw it our way.

As a result, the federal bench is peppered with men and women who are noted for ideology over ability. Romney did not manifest the kind of mind that would have respected the difference. I think President Obama displays a higher regard for what used to be known as "judicial temperament."

⊨⧧ ⧧⊨

The people who went to the polls were voting for or against something and presumably believed they understood what they were doing.

What was it?

Let us note, regret, and pass beyond the truth that some opposition to President Obama is racial. The better point is also the larger one. The country as a whole elected an African American president and then re-elected him in difficult circumstances. This should be a matter of pride and hope.

Some others no doubt voted against the president because they felt his administration had begun to display the body language of a stalled enterprise. Opinions will vary on how much of this should be laid to him, how much to fickle circumstance, and how much to the relentless effort of Congressional foes to sabotage his work. Fairly or unfairly, voters could have felt that blame should be fixed where credit would be taken if matters were in a better state.

Anti-Romney voters could have rejected him for a dozen reasons. His campaign reeked of dishonesty. His expressed view of the American public was a caricature. His philosophy of government was a mystery because he intentionally made it one. If he really was a conservative, he was a ham-handed and myopic one.

But what about the affirmative view of choice? What about the voters who were selecting something they wanted?

A vote for Republicans or Democrats has traditionally been viewed as a vote for smaller or bigger government. This formulation is no longer apt. Our central government will remain huge no matter who has the White House. Several Republican presidents rank high among architects of larger government enterprise.

The useful differences between the two parties would have more to do with priorities for effort, with breadth of initiative, and with appropriate restraint. Republicans would be the party more wary of the destructive power of taxation and less ready to view government as a problem-solver of first resort.

There is a useful place for this point of view in our national deliberation of ends and means. But it has been lost or, to speak more precisely, abandoned by those in control of the Republican Party today. They have overdosed on a toxic mixture of political extremism, intolerant religion, and cultural bigotry.

Sad to say, some voters wanted to choose exactly that. But let's hope that most Republican voters merely wanted to express the not unreasonable view that our government's reach has exceeded its grasp and its ability to pay the bills in a responsible way.

And those of us who chose the Obama ticket? I'm guessing most of us feel that the greater inclusivity of the Democratic Party is right as a matter of principle—and far more realistic as an approach to governing a country where diversity is on a steady march.

⊨⊹ ⊹⊨

Confession time: during my working years, I was a journalist.

My mother never knew. I told her I was a piano player in a bawdy house. I thought this would suit her better than knowing that her son was a member of the media.

But even given the public's low regard for my old trade (Mom was not alone by any means), I remember it fondly. Thus I am vexed by some of what passes for journalism today.

Of the hucksters at Fox News we can only say that they are—well, hucksters.

And surely I am not the only one who would like shelter from the widespread blizzard of postelection analysis. How many ways are there to say that people who favored the Democratic point of view prevailed through the cunning tactic of voting in greater numbers? And how many times must it be said?

I am reminded of the job description for journalists: They sit on the sidelines of the battlefield until the fighting is over. Then the journalists ride down onto the battlefield and shoot the wounded.

WHO KIDNAPPED THE REAL REPUBLICANS?
JANUARY 7, 2013

I got a letter from Uncle Barlow the other day. He's had some time on his hands since the Ladies' Auxiliary of the First Barlow Church discovered he did a little bootlegging in his youth. He's been mostly staying home and out of sight, because whenever he goes out in public, they try to save him from his sins. He's used the time to give some extra thought to political trends. Here's what he had to say:

Dear Nephew,

Well, darned if we don't have ourselves a big political mixup here in Barlow County. The way Millie over at the library says it, the tides are changing.

You see, the Buncombe brothers decided to set up a drag race out on the old bypass. Sheriff Poole got wind of it and figured he'd go out there and shut them down. Ordinarily he wouldn't have paid it any mind, but it was an election year, and he had a young fella giving him some competition. Sheriff Poole thought he ought to put on some extra show.

Trouble is, the Buncombe brothers are better drivers than he is, and they have faster cars. When they saw him coming, they just lit out. They took him through a hairpin turn on the back side of Barlow's Knob, and he lost control of his cruiser and landed in the low end of Lester Hobgood's hog pen. The muck in that pen was so deep, the sheriff's car fetched up short and sharp, and the plastic Jesus flew off his dashboard and gave him a shiner.

Now, the sheriff felt a little self-conscious about campaigning with a shiner he got from a plastic Jesus in a hog pen. So, some of the old money boys around here told him not to bother too much, just to relax -- said they'd buy him some extra advertising, even some TV time, and he'd cruise right in.

But he didn't. The young fella beat him, and now he and the old money boys are trying to figure out what the heck happened to them.

Kind of reminds me of those Republican folks up there in Washington, since they lost the presidential election, and some seats in Congress, and a good deal of their strut. Every time I turn on the TV, I see something about them thrashing around and trying to figure out what to do now. Mostly, it looks like to me, they cause trouble, especially over there in the U.S. House of Representatives. That Speaker fellow, Boehner, has his hands full just trying to maintain an appearance that the inmates are not in charge of the asylum.

Now, I think some of those folks have a lot of brass even calling themselves Republicans at all. I mean, I could call myself a Chinaman, but that wouldn't make me one. I'm thinking about the real Republicans -- the kind we used to have. We need to have them back again.

I say this even though I'm a Democrat. Always have been. I kind of like the way Democrats think that folks should get a helping hand if they need one. Of course the bad news about the Democrats has always been that they can get pretty frisky with taxes.

The good thing about the Republicans was that they were apt to be a little more careful about taxing other people's money. The bad news about them was that if you fell down, they might be a little bit too apt just to leave you where you landed.

It used to be that if you put the Republicans and the Democrats in together, and they each got to have a little say about how they government should run, they sort of balanced each other out, and the government went along pretty well for the most part, over the longer time.

But nowadays, when it comes to getting the government to run on more or less the right track, it looks to me like some of these so-called Republicans have been about as useful as tits on a bull, if you will forgive my language.

About half the time, even with all the big problems that need to be talked about, they keep getting hung up on religion and sex and what women should be allowed to do with their private parts. (If they start offering to make rules about what I can do with my Johnson, I'm going to be peeved, let me tell you.)

The other half of the time they are trying to make President Obama look bad. It's like they don't really care that the people elected him. The other day that senator from Kentucky, that McConnell fellow, got so twisted around trying to make the president look bad that he wound up talking against his own bill. I'm not sure I understand how that happened. But come to think of it, neither did Senator McConnell, apparently, so I guess I shouldn't feel so bad.

I just don't understand how some of these so-called Republicans can hate the president so bad. They seem to think everything is just personally about him. I swear, I hope the Almighty doesn't choose President Obama to announce the time of the second coming. Those Republicans over there in the House of Representatives will vote to change the schedule.

I decided I would take it up with Millie over at the library. She understands some of these things a lot better. And I'm going to tell what she said just the way she said it. Millie has more words than I do.

I said: "Millie, how come some of these Republicans hate the president so bad?"

And Millie said: "Well, partly it's because they're confused and alarmed, maybe even a little afraid. The times and the attitudes of the electorate are changing in ways that seem threatening to some of them. They don't like the message, so they're attacking the messenger.

"And then you have bunches of extremists who are bent on having their way even if a majority don't want it -- and even if the consequences don't square with what they claim are their principles. Take a look at the fine print of some of the legislation that got passed during all the blathering over the so-called fiscal cliff. Republicans stuck in some language authorizing continued spending -- which is already in the millions -- on courtroom defenses of the anti-gay Defense of Marriage Act. That act already is in deep trouble in the courts, and is being abandoned politically even by some who initially voted for it. But the Republican extremists won't let go. Talk about wasteful spending. Talk about piling hypocrisy on top of stupidity.

"We are likely to see more of this in the fight over raising the debt ceiling. Some in Congress are saying they won't raise the ceiling unless the White House agrees to certain policies they want. Of course, if they don't raise the ceiling, the government will default on its credit obligations -- obligations that legally apply to Republicans as well as Democrats -- an the whole country will be harmed. Republican extremists are threatening to damage the welfare of the American people if the President won't give them policy concessions they can't win by appropriate legislative means.

"It's a damn poor show. Officials who have accepted a sworn obligation to govern in the interests of all the people are trying to sabotage the work of a duly elected president. I suppose they will eventually learn they can't turn back the tide by shouting at it. But in the meantime they seem ready to do a lot of damage."

Well, that's how Millie sees it, and I have to say I think she's got some pretty good points. The kind of Republicans we used to have -- the kind who had some thoughtful and useful things to say—have gotten to be about as welcome up there in Washington as ex-wives at a family reunion.

I have to go now. I promised to go over and play some checkers with Sheriff Poole. (We still call him that. It's kind of a courtesy.) He needs some company and maybe a little Dutch Uncle advice. He just can't stand the notion that the people turned him out. He's begun to talk a little crazy. He's saying the young fella beat him by promising to treat poor folks the same way he'd treat the big money boys -- as if there was something wrong with that. And he's started muttering about how maybe the young fella isn't really even a legal resident of Barlow County.

On the other hand, maybe with a little time, he'll mend. He did put the plastic Jesus back on his dashboard."

Sincerely,

Your Uncle Barlow

GUN NUTS
FEBRUARY 11, 2013

When we Americans crank up our gun-control fights, we display a marked capacity for cockeyed behavior. Hear US Senator Mitch McConnell in an e-mail to constituents (we will return later to the salutation's veiled insinuation):

> Dear Patriot,
>
> You and I are literally surrounded. The gun grabbers in the Senate are about to launch an all-out assault on the Second Amendment. On your rights.
>
> On Your freedom.
>
> Just the other night President Obama urged them to act. And then he went one step further, spelling out 23 executive orders he will take to get your guns.

The message continues in this vein. Even by the standards of fear-mongering, this is gamy stuff. President Obama and his legislative allies have not offered to "grab" anything. If fair-minded people may consider some particulars debatable—and some do—the president's agenda is not extreme. It displays not a whit of contempt for the Constitution. It is a measured attempt to address problems of gun violence.

Sen. McConnell, who may face a reelection challenge from the right, has extra reasons for choosing to incite his constituents rather than lead them. But he is far from being alone in going for red-meat rhetoric on this issue. Images of jack-booted government are common coin among opponents of gun control.

What prompts these extremes of language and attitude?

Greed, in some instances.

Assuming for the sake of argument that the average family has no pressing need of an imitation combat rifle, it is reasonable to ask: Who has a vested interest in protecting the manufacture and sale of imitation combat rifles—and Saturday night specials, and other dubious weaponry?

It is reasonable to answer: People who manufacture and sell dubious weaponry.

Enter the National Rifle Association, a gun industry lobby posing as a guardian of citizens' rights. Lobbyists who want to keep their jobs must demonstrate clout. The NRA shrinks from no opportunity, however bizarre. Not long ago it buffaloed the Wisconsin legislature away from a proposal to ban loaded firearms from the public galleries of the legislative chambers.

The NRA is loud and clever on behalf of gun manufacturers. But it also is openly ruthless and, from time to time, downright absurd. (Its website contains an enemies list that includes the YWCA and Pam Dawber, an aging alumna of the seventies TV sitcom *Mork and Mindy*). All this for a business that is—in its sales to civilian markets—a very small player in the American economy.

How can one rogue organization command the attention of the whole country on behalf of a fringe industry?

It doesn't. Quite apart from the ranting of the NRA, gun control proposals strike their own chords among Americans. They raise questions of privacy and property rights in parts of the country where gun ownership is an ordinary and harmless feature of the common culture.

And they call to mind of one of government's lower habits. Unable—or unwilling—to do what they should, officials may simply do whatever they can and pronounce the result sufficient. Sensible people may conclude that some gun control proposals fit this pattern all too neatly: Unable to control or deter the violent few, the government settles for the expedient of encumbering the innocent many. Few of us require an explanation of the old gibe, "Close enough for government work."

Even so, reasonable and promising gun-control measures are available for the taking. They may suffer in public debate precisely to the degree that they are not extreme. Measured voices are difficult to hear in a storm of shouting.

Nowadays, wild-eyed gun advocates are gladly sheltering in the larger right-wing assault on Obama administration policies and on President Obama personally. (The NRA sponsored an ad calling the president "elitist" and caricaturing the protective measures required by law for his young daughters.)

In this lamentable context, Sen. McConnell sets out to lather up the home folks. He and those who agree with him are "patriots." People who disagree with him are…well, something else.

We may be reminded of the eighteenth-century sage Samuel Johnson. He said, "Patriotism is the last refuge of a scoundrel."

UNCLE BARLOW MEETS THE NRA
FEBRUARY 22, 2013

I got a letter from Uncle Barlow the other day. He has become a bit of celebrity down there where he lives in Barlow County, and that is bringing new pressures on him from his friends and neighbors. Here's what he had to say.

Dear Nephew,

Well, I am surely in a pickle. I think I told you that the Ladies' Genealogical Society was doing a personal history of Barlow County. Well, wouldn't you know, while they were doing all that digging into my family history, they discovered my full, formal legal name, which I believe you probably don't know, since I have always kept pretty quiet about it.

I was christened Pierre Gustav Toutant Beauregard Barlow. You see, my daddy was a Civil War Buff, and I guess this Beauregard fellow was some kind of general back then. You can probably understand why I've always just gone by plain old "Barlow."

Anyhow, when that ladies' bunch found out about it, they kind of decided that somebody named after a big general with a Frenchy-sounding name must be some sort of special deal, in genealogical terms, and they started wanting to get ever so much better acquainted with me. They started wanting me to "participate" in their "discussions."

And that's where I made my mistake, because I said right out plain, "Discussions of what?" Now, the Ladies' Genealogical Society is pretty much the same bunch as the Barlow County Ladies' Civic Action Committee. About the time I said "discussions of what?" they were going through kind of a slow spell and looking around for something new to be active about. Some of them began talking about my family's "military history." Pretty soon they were wanting me to give them a talk about gun control. And durn me, I couldn't figure a way to get out of it.

Since I didn't know anything about gun control, I started poking around and reading about it. I got mighty confused mighty quick, let me tell you. I read all this stuff about how sportsmen and hunters needed to be concerned because the gun-controllers wanted to come and take their guns away. I do a little deer hunting from time to time, so I figured maybe I needed to be concerned, too.

But then I read on some more and, near as I can tell, mostly the kind of thing that the gun-control folks want to regulate is fake combat rifles and great big high-capacity magazines—20 shots and more, some of them.

Now, I don't know much about gun control, but I do know something about hunting, and I am here to tell you this: If you can get a deer to stand still while you shoot at it 20 times, you don't need a gun of any kind. You could hunt that sucker with a baseball bat.

Being thoroughly confused, which I was, I thought I should stop looking at secondary sources. (Millie over at the library calls them that.) I thought I should go directly to the horse's mouth, so to speak. I started looking first-hand at the stuff put out by the National Rifle Association.

Now, the first thing that got my attention was their head man, the one who looks like he just sat bare-assed on a hair brush. Wayne LaPierre is his name. Some of the stuff he had to say was so nutty, I wondered for a minute if I'd messed up and stumbled across some comedian. But no, there he was, right in all the official stuff the NRA puts out.

By this time I was a country mile beyond confusion. I went over to the library and asked Millie to help me out.

Millie told me hell no he's not a comedian. He's serious as a heart attack. She waved a paper at me and said I had to read it. Said it was an article he'd written somewhere.

In the article he said the president's financial policies could lead to a great big national breakdown: "Nobody knows if or when the fiscal collapse will come, but if the country is broke there likely won't be enough money to pay for police protection. And the American people know it.

"Hurricanes. Tornadoes. Riots. Terrorists. Gangs. Lone criminals. These are the perils we are sure to face—not just maybe. It is not paranoia to buy a gun. It's survival."

Millie said, "If he believes that bafflegab, he's a fool, and if he doesn't believe it, he's a con man." I kind of asked her which one she thought he was, since I hadn't had much luck making heads or tails of him any which way.

She said, "Keep reading the claptrap." She pointed to a place farther in down in the article where he said the only way to keep the country from going straight to the dickens was to strengthen the NRA. He asked for donations of $20 or $50 or even $1,000. He said he and his bunch were going to work hard to recruit a lot more members. He called them "lovers of freedom."

Millie said "Lovers of freedom, hell!" (She gets kind of salty when she gets worked up.) "He wants to collect more dues. That's his message: The sky is falling! Send me money! It's a wonder he doesn't offer a free bottle of snake oil with every membership. And we've got members of Congress who listen to that guy."

Well, I just have to say, I don't know why anybody would listen to him, much less send him money. And so I still don't know what to say to that ladies' bunch about all this gun control argument, except that they might get themselves about the same grade of discussion in the secure wing over at the home.

Maybe I can talk them into being interested in something else. And in the meantime, I guess I'll just have to hope they don't find out that NRA fellow has a Frenchy-sounding name.

Sincerely,

Your Uncle Barlow

CHRISTIAN FOOTBALL?
APRIL 6, 2013

We are selective about living up to our principles. All of us. We don't judge books by their covers—but we notice that the man down the street wears terribly cheap clothes. His carelessness of appearance must say something about him. Mustn't it?

We believe that people's marital relationships are personal and private—but we're aware that a colleague's daughter is including the word "obey" in her upcoming marriage vows. In this day and time? Really?

We admire a willingness to question tradition and try new ways—but the couple on the next block are so militantly avante garde in their parenting that we wonder (along with others, we learn in neighborhood chitchat) if their children are getting anything like proper guidance.

We are selective about living up to our principles. All of us.

So we should be cautious of casting stones at Tim Tebow for being selective about his. Tebow is a professional football quarterback.

He is also an assertively self-proclaimed Christian who plays a violent game on the Christian Sabbath for sums of money surpassing a widow's mite by tens of millions.

When public figures make a point of calling themselves Christians, we infer purpose beyond a mere declaration of personal belief. We anticipate—and are meant to—evangelistic behavior and conservative views on such litmus-test social issues as abortion.

Tebow fills this bill. He is such a vivid example that, in some circles, his name is more than one kind of household word. His posture in kneeling for prayer on the football field has been widely called "Tebowing." He finally trademarked the term. Just wanted to be sure it's "used in the right way," he said.

Of course Tebow is not alone in dragging religion into secular venues. Nowadays we have Christian celebrities and celebrity Christians and even (may we say "heaven help us" at this juncture?) Christian politicians.

And there's the local parson who offers up a prayer before the big high-school game. Or the mom-and-pop enterprise down the street that calls itself a Christian business. (My town has a Christian furniture store.)

Want Christian sex toys? The Internet offers dozens of sources. How about Christian professional wrestling? Two full-blown circuits are grappling for God.

People who strike religious poses to sell dildos can simply be considered beneath comment.

On other points: Appearances suggest that Tebow may be utterly and terribly sincere—a naïve young man who sees no presumption in claiming to be a brand name for prayer. Benefit of the doubt also can be given to that local parson. He is a man of the cloth, after all, even if he sees no irony in inviting divine attention to a contest that is the antithesis of turning the other cheek.

Perhaps that Christian merchant means only to say that he won't cheat or gouge. And no offense is meant, surely, by people who pray aloud in restaurants. Or by cashiers who say "God bless you" to customers whose religious sensibilities they cannot know.

By the bigshots who use celebrity to push their chosen form of religion, and by the ordinary folks who plaster muddy, tattered "Jesus saves" bumper stickers on their cars, we are reminded that even good intentions can produce bad results. A religion-on-every-corner ethic adulterates values. Casual displays of religiosity, like other rote declarations of affection, trivialize their object.

People of faith should regret this. And others would be mistaken to consider it only an intramural matter. When religion is trivialized, a bar is lowered. Over it step people who are willing to put a religious veneer on secular agendas. Yes, alas, a few of our politicians do seem actually to believe that God is on their side. The rest, we may reasonably suspect, see advantage in claiming a divine mandate for their opinions. It marvelously short-circuits any obligation to deal forthrightly with differing points of view. I'm right, you're wrong, end of discussion.

We are all diminished when the adulteration of values becomes a value in itself. And the country is sadly polarized when people—innocently or otherwise—confuse their personal outlook with revealed truth.

WHO OWNS MARRIAGE?
MAY 27, 2013

This is a true story.

He is seventy-one; she is seventy. They have been together four years and have fashioned a shared life that is to them precious. They would have entered a conventional marriage, but for a tangle of legalistic reasons, they could not. Instead, they undertook a commitment ceremony. A clergyman heard their vows to stay together for life; he blessed their union, and he said: "I proclaim that they are united to one another in a holy covenant."

They are thrilled. The ceremony put a seal on what matters most to them. The difference from a conventional, legal marriage is peripheral.

Friends and family are thrilled as well. Notably, they are thrilled in the same way. They agree with the clergyman's declaration that the essence of marriage is in the quality of a couple's commitment.

One friend put it crisply: "Who cares what the government thinks?"

Polls confirm what that quip suggests. Attitudes toward the definition of marriage are changing. Some fear that less value is being accorded the traditional man/woman relationship, sanctioned in law, as the foundation of the traditional family. This is a view through the wrong end of the telescope. A better one is that more value is being allowed for other forms of lifelong commitment.

This liberalization of attitude takes place amid the national debate of gay marriage. They are, of course, connected. Yet most Americans, being heterosexual, have no direct, personal stake in the institution of gay marriage. What, then, could have caused the tide of opinion to turn at this juncture toward a broader definition of wedlock?

Possibly, injury to a sense of fair play and elementary justice. Possibly, in the debate of gay marriage, the extreme right has discredited its own writ.

Few of us would dispute the need for government to protect public health and define the parameters of taxation and property ownership. But the epicenter of opposition to gay marriage has been located elsewhere. It has been focused in highly selective moralisms, in citations of debatable and dubiously relevant religious tradition, in silly predictions that civilization will crumble if persons of the same gender are permitted to formalize loving relationships.

And the larger context is not lost on attentive observers. Doomsaying on gay marriage comes from the same quarters that produce, on the issue of abortion, discussion of vaginal probes and "legitimate" rape. In this, self-styled apostles of limited government have revealed a willingness for government to invade the most intimate aspects of life.

Mean-spirited extremes against gay marriage have attracted attention to the extremes themselves. As a dog's breakfast of bigotry and hypocrisy is offered up, many Americans are declining to partake. They may have friends or loved ones in relationships that are not less precious for lying outside traditional norms. Or they may simply feel that, if the government presumes to define love, it presumes too much.

At a level of plain common sense that underpins American public attitudes at their best, vigilante politics on the right may have reawakened this awareness: Politicians on every side share a defining trait. They are glad to hold power over the rest of us. Some of them are willing to take as much of it as we'll cede.

Scaremongering is not leadership. It is a herding tactic. Scaremongering on intensely personal issues has revealed a disrespect for boundaries that protect us all.

Appearances suggest a backlash. In any event, an attitude is emerging: Valid marital commitments are not limited to what the government of the moment has been willing to sanction.

YOU DON'T MATTER
JULY 17, 2013

I looked forward to the dinner. The menu was inviting, the dining room gracious. They suggested the meal could be a bit of an experience. I hoped so, anyway. It was part of a long-planned trip that was to be a once-in-a-lifetime thing for us.

Not much about the fellow at a nearby table was noticeable, except that the mild disarray of his clothing suggested calculation along with carelessness—a bit of bohemian style not fully abandoned in middle age.

He became noticeable when he began to complain roughly about his dinner and then made a show of sending it back to the kitchen. The servers acquiesced. The maître d' nodded and smiled as the man declared that he was himself a chef and simply could not eat the food that had been served to him. Apologies were made, new servings were brought, and the rest of us were able to return to our dinners without further interruption.

On a second night, the complainer repeated his performance. Those of us within earshot paused while servers hovered and the chef himself appeared. Again apologies were made, new servings brought, and our meals permitted to continue.

The man was, of course, a bully. He abused dining-room workers who were in no position to fight back. He was also something else. To the other diners whose evenings he interrupted, he was extravagantly rude.

The episodes irritated a particular nerve in me. I am, by background and some aspects of attitude, a Southerner. I love the lilt and resonance of the region's many accents. I love the lyric sense that nourishes its distinguished literature. I love the gumbo of cultures and the rainbow of music, from blues and jazz to the hints of bagpipe in the Scots-Irish tunes of the Appalachians.

And one more attitude marks me out as a Southerner: I am hypersensitive to considerations of courtesy. By this I do not mean mandarin systems of etiquette. I mean simply that a person should not knowingly discomfort another.

A lifetime of residential relocation has taught me that others may agree in principle but differ sharply in practice.

In the Northeast some idiom seemed quite coarse. I had to learn that it was not meant to attack or insult me. It was just a way of speaking. I had also to learn in those regions that my own manners could seem to be a fancy pose. When, as a young man, I first said "sir" and "ma'am" to figures of authority or respect, some thought I was mocking them.

When I moved to the Midwest, my new acquaintances did not view me as a Southerner. To them I was an Easterner. Our conversational rhythms were very different. I thought they could take a long time to answer a simple question. They thought I was brusque in twitching to wrap up before they had finished giving information I'd asked for.

North, South, East, West: ideas of manners varied widely.

As a guest at one family's Sunday dinner, I brought the entire meal to a brief halt by putting sugar in my iced tea. They had never seen it done. They thought my behavior was an unkind comment on the beverage they had served me.

I came to brace myself especially for funerals and weddings, where in my estimation accepted norms could range from odd to ghastly.

Whatever the variation in particulars, two attitudes are common:

- Rules of courtesy are quite specific. Polite people must do certain things and must refrain from doing certain others.
- One's own customs are standard, and everyone else's are—in the usual euphemism—"different."

The years have rigorously disabused me of that second notion. The principle of the thing is what I care about. In my view, the effort of common courtesy is a gesture of respect for others. Failures of courtesy are thus the opposite. They amount to saying, "You don't matter."

Hence I take more than a passing interest in public displays of rudeness. Even small ones, like that of the dawdler who queues beside a wall-mounted menu for several minutes but bothers to read it and make up his mind only when he has reached the head of the line. Or the grocery shopper who must tidy every corner of her purse before moving on from the cashier.

We can give these offenders benefit of the doubt. They may be only carelessly indifferent to the interests of the people around them.

But the boor in the dining room was one of the sort who seem to perceive some point or pleasure in throwing their weight around.

He was quite clearly aware of his impact on other diners. (And he did clean up his act when they—peers—began to stare him down.)

Rudeness at a focused, personal level stirs a kind of distrust in me. If you tell me I don't matter, I take you at your word and keep my guard up even when you are all smiles. Respect is a Humpty-Dumpty kind of thing. If it's gone, it's gone.

And with age I have become less willing even to appear tolerant of discourtesy. I hope that I never return rudeness for rudeness. However, I am no longer likely to smile through it—or give leeway to those who actually announce that they mean to impinge on my time, space, or comfort: I hope you don't mind if I...

In fact I do mind, and nowadays I probably will say so. Often this visibly surprises the advertisers, who seem to feel entitled to the sufferance of others. They expect to enjoy all their own prerogatives and some of mine, too.

I prefer to hang on to mine...

Thank you very much.

FROM NORTH CAROLINA, WITH CHAGRIN

AUGUST 20, 2013

I live in North Carolina.

Nowadays, this admission is embarrassing. You may understand if you've been watching television comics. Among them my state has become an object of ridicule. Or perhaps you've been reading the national press. There, my state is being described with astonishment and regret.

These portrayals involve a certain amount of caricature. The comedians do it for effect. The journalists and commentators are simply using some necessary shorthand.

So let me supply a few details from a firsthand perspective. And as I do, let me mention with bewilderment that I knew our new governor, Pat McCrory, face-to-face for many years. I was a working journalist. He was the longtime mayor of my hometown. I knew him—back then—to be a bright, knowledgeable public official with an open-minded awareness of his obligation to serve all the citizens of his city.

Gov. McCrory—in office less than a year—is a Republican. Not long ago Republicans also gained control of both houses of our legislature for the first time in more than one hundred years. Together, in just a few months, they have loosed a tide of deeply conservative change in state law and policy.

In the interest of full disclosure, I should say that I find many of these changes objectionable and some of them downright appalling, especially as they afflict women, poor people, and minorities. This, however, is not the whole of my point. Perhaps one example will illustrate.

Among the new laws is one restricting access to voting. It sets stringent standards of photo identification for would-be voters. The law has stirred up waves of criticism. Gov. McCrory has stubbornly defended it and decried "scare tactics" from the "extreme left."

This kind of language from Pat McCrory baffles and dismays me. It goes to a level of demagoguery that should be beneath any decent man. The fact is that this voter law has occasioned vigorous concern among people of moderate mind and informed perspective.

To these citizens of North Carolina, their governor gives the back of his hand.

And there is the snapshot that reveals the new character of our public affairs.

While North Carolina politics and policy have wandered left and right in modern times, the center line has remained just that. The heart's blood of this state's civic ethic has been a kind of sleeves-up, centrist pragmatism. Our latter-day conservative revolution is wrong because it is fundamentally and knowingly out of tune with the long-manifest outlook of the North Carolina electorate.

So, how did that electorate come to elevate public officials who would break faith with their obligation to represent all the people? The answer comes in two parts.

The first part has to do with the influence of big money. One rich man, who now holds a high office in the McCrory administration, for years systematically backed conservative causes and candidates. Eventually they prevailed in controlling numbers.

And as Republicans mounted the march of the bag men, they were aided by a second factor at work in North Carolina. Many of us don't vote, and many who do are not paying attention. In this we create a vacuum for big money to fill.

Of course Republican leaders would not agree with me. They would deny favoring an aristocracy of wealth willing to buy power to which it is not rightly entitled. They would deny betraying an ethical obligation to serve all the people without regard to party affiliation. They would deny that our governor has lost his bearings and that our legislature has sunk to whooping through jack-leg law just because it can.

They might say they are clearing government-made debris off the road to a better future for North Carolinians. They might say they are creating a good, conservative, business-friendly climate to help North Carolina's economy grow and its citizens prosper. I think they might say they are creating a new brand name for North Carolina as a state that is hospitable to enterprise and ripe with opportunity for all who are willing to work.

They might ask why they should be deterred in this by coverage in the national press and the antics of a few TV jokesters.

I would say they should be deterred because the nation can see in the press the whole truth: Much of what's happening in this state has nothing to do with government streamlining or economic stimulation. It has to do with fat-cat manipulation, bully-boy politics, and narrow-minded social attitudes that are directly at odds with the obligations of proper government to a populace of diverse needs. With purchased political power, a band of partisans has forced their pet agenda on the rest of us.

I say all this from a point of view that is not within a country mile of the "extreme left." (And I say the new voter law is a high-tech poll tax.) And I do not think all those TV jokesters can be dismissed as mere funnymen. Their jibes at North Carolina are a warning that our Republican bosses are indeed creating a new brand name for this state, and that it could be "Laughingstock."

Advocates of plutocracy are not limiting their attention to North Carolina. Some of them tried to buy the White House for Mitt Romney (who, in a little-noted voice message, urged business leaders to "explain" election issues to their employees.)

And Americans from shore to shore belong to that vast power bloc that determines the outcome of many elections: people who don't vote and don't bother to remain informed.

In North Carolina, while the boodle boys were arranging for our state government to become household staff to the upper crust, many of us were looking the other way. We now have a lot of work to do to reclaim what's ours.

Let's hope people elsewhere wake up before the same thing happens to them.

FREE LUNCH FOR YOU
SEPTEMBER 20, 2013

I dislike professional evangelists—and not only the con artists who are in it for the money. I'm troubled also by others who may, in their way, be utterly and terribly sincere.

They are not offering free lunch, exactly, but they do advertise a kind of cheap grace. Each claims to offer a grand "Open Sesame," an ultimate password. They reduce the mysteries of spirituality to the idiom of a late-night kitchen gadget commercial: "Just follow these simple steps…"

And—when the preaching reaches a crescendo—if the exhortation to follow a higher call begins to sound like an exhortation to follow me, I don't think my ears are playing tricks.

In any case, I was predisposed to be annoyed by an article about Richard Dawkins.

His enterprise fits the standard parameters. He claims to know the only right view of human spirituality. If you veer from his charted path, he says, you will go astray. He travels to preach. He sells books. He has a foundation, and, yes, he will be glad to take your check.

He does differ from some of his brethren in one particular: he is an atheist. If he is not the first atheist to turn pro, he is notably enterprising. He is a prolific author, speaker, and blogger. His website offers T-shirts, water bottles, a newsletter, and a Twitter feed.

A Google scamper through his work does not equip me for a balanced review; however, a couple of specifics seem pertinent in considering his type and making our way to a larger point.

He begins from a premise that reality consists only of what science can measure. He then ventures to apply a yardstick to infinity and points out that the results are droll.

But of course in disguising his conclusion as his premise, he simply evades the essential question altogether. As a scientist and former Oxford professor, he does, surely, know better. A first-year student of logic would be faulted in this for a lack of intellectual rigor. In everyday language, he would be charged with shucking and jiving.

Asked by an interviewer what he would say if he met God after his own death, Dawkins replied "The first thing I would say is, well, which one are you? Are you Zeus? Are you Thor? Are you Baal? Are you Mithras? Are you Yahweh?"

Here he is shucking and jiving again. He was asked how he would react if he discovered that his own beliefs were false. An inventory of other people's beliefs does not constitute an answer of any sort. It is a classic non sequitur.

And as an array of ideas, his response is the bottom of a slob's shoe closet. It represents a jumble of religion, myth, and cultic mumbo-jumbo. It is as if Dawkins had been offered a serving of fruit, and he asked if it would include apples, doorknobs, stepladders, or soup spoons. He purports to compare concepts that are not sensibly comparable.

If Dawkins does not know this, he is remarkably ill-informed. And again, if he does know it—well, I need not go further toward accusing him of ignorance, flabby thinking, and rhetorical sleight of hand. A variety of his peers, including several distinguished scientists, have already done that.

All my fun at Dawkins' expense is highly selective. Enough of it. The larger point is that the professional Christian and the professional atheist are in similar games. Both deal in caricature.

The anti-religionists peddle caricatures that are easy to ridicule.

The styled and blow-dried Bible-wavers peddle caricatures that are easy to swallow: Why, grasping the ultimate truth of the universe is as easy as falling off a log. Just praise the Lord, catch the vibe. and put another dollar in the pot.

The dissemination of spiritual junk food is not inconsequential. The appetite for it rises, I think, from two sources. One is an earnest inner desire of most people to know what is right and what is true. The other is a hankering for simple answers, for quick fixes. It is cousin to the yen that sustains a market year after year for fad diets.

Religious hokum would be harder to peddle were it not for a widespread climate of Biblical ignorance. This deficit is lamentable in its own right. Wholly apart from considerations of faith, Judeo-Christian scriptures are among the foundation documents of Western culture. Yet our systems of education routinely grant credentials of literacy to people who have never read them.

Meanwhile, hokum milks money from the gullible, aggravates cultural divisions, and infects our politics.

POLITICS AS HOLY WAR
NOVEMBER 13, 2013

I am thinking these days about two particular friends of mine. They are middle-aged men, professional men both. They are family men and homeowners. They are diligent citizens, kind and caring human beings—just the sort we'd all be glad to have to have, say, as neighbors.

My two friends are homosexual. They have been together in a loving, monogamous relationship for twenty-six years. They live in a state that now permits same-sex unions, and they are about to be married.

They are on my mind in a bittersweet way. I'm delighted that they are finally able to place upon their relationship the seal that so many of us take for granted. But I'm sad that they have had to wait so very long to be allowed this opportunity.

Other homosexual Americans continue waiting, as the rest of the country snarls through decisions about the posture of law and politics toward personal matters. Our civic conversation is roiled by dubious moralizing and overcooked religiosity. Religious factions offer themselves as voting blocs, and their leaders offer themselves as power brokers. Our politicians stir the pot as they declaim about preserving family values and protecting marriage. Some of them seem actually to believe that marriage is under attack and that family values can be usefully framed in the vocabulary of politics. Others are only pandering.

Toxic mixtures of religion and politics are not new. Consider Prohibition. And one's definition of appropriate preacher behavior can depend on one's point of view. I might have favored the clergy who energized the American Revolution. I did favor the ones who energized the American civil rights movement.

Still, it appears to me that the likes of John Hagee and Jerry Falwell have crossed into mere partisanship. And in any case, the nation does seem to have been running an especially high fever for a while. The sanctimonious right has contorted Republican politics with a striking irony. In it, the supposed apostles of limited government labor to push government into the most intimate aspects of personal life. Political pandering has reached such lows that a sitting president, the second President Bush, endorsed the crackpot notion of writing a Judeo-Christian definition or marriage into the Constitution of the United States.

It's a strong brew, this notion that some political opinions (and the people who hold them) are morally superior to other political opinions (and the people who hold those.) Some of our leaders are bingeing on it. Under the influence, they have turned politics into a kind of holy war across a broad front. A faction in Congress has relentlessly connived to undermine the work of a duly elected president. In one revealing extreme, they shut down the government rather than tolerate the implementation of a duly enacted law.

And so the rest of us are subjected to the obverse of what our system of government is supposed to be about. It is supposed to shelter and accommodate competing values. But Washington's hotheads of the moment want to use it to enshrine some values and drive others out. In other times and places, there was a word for people who took the law into their own hands and trampled opposition down. They were called vigilantes. The analogy is extreme, but it is not irrelevant.

This spree of intolerance won't last, and we must hope that other politicians will then forego tit for tat. (My compatriots on the leftward side of things have shown that we are not above taking our own taste of the brew. But that's a discussion for another time.) My particular hope is for broader recognition that heedless commerce between religion and government is dangerously foolhardy. Preachers who want churches to elevate politics of their choosing invite politicians to think they might elevate churches of their choosing.

Meanwhile, in one corner of the country, my two friends have finally escaped having dogma enforced upon them through civil law. Godspeed to them, and may many others follow.

THE POPE IN OUR EAR
JANUARY 15, 2014

I t is common to suppose that human progress, if represented on a graph, would be a steadily ascending line. But some writers say otherwise. They say the line would be a curving one, sometimes ascending and sometimes descending along a horizontal axis.

They see matters this way: Smarter machines and bigger buildings don't amount to human progress, because machines and buildings aren't human. If we consider, instead, modes of thought and systems of values, we see that some ancient societies were quite sophisticated—and were already so at the earliest moments we are able to discern. Yet the value systems of some later societies have been crude. On the whole, we have not become better human beings. We have only become better *equipped* human beings. If our modern tools and methods have empowered us to achieve great good, they have also armed us to do great harm. Our instinct for the latter has not diminished as we've achieved what we call progress.

All of which brings me to a major treatise by Pope Francis. (Full disclosure: I have never been a member of the Roman Catholic Church.) Commentators of various persuasions have cherry-picked his long message for validation of their own views. At the admitted risk of doing the same, I would make the following points.

Only one part of the Pope's message was devoted to his much-discussed condemnation of trickle-down capitalism. In it, he denounced a financial system that "rules rather than serves." He cautioned against "crude and naive trust in the goodness of those wielding economic power and in the sacralized workings of the prevailing economic system." He warned that our times are "pervaded—by consumerism" that produces "…a complacent yet covetous heart, the feverish pursuit of frivolous pleasures, and a blunted conscience."

Viewed whole, the Pope's treatise is a blueprint for the role of the Catholic Church in the world. It touches on a sweeping variety of topics: economics, politics, poverty, technology, racism, gender equality, and more. It is a thoughtful and balanced work. It is notably well informed on the ways of the secular world.

He cautions us against abdicating personal responsibility in favor of institutional norms. He begins, of course, with the Roman Catholic Church. He challenges the church to channel its customs and methods more effectively toward service "rather than for her self-preservation." He worries that the church "is unhealthy from being confined and from clinging to its own security."

Pope Francis clearly means these admonitions for other institutions as well, so let me now borrow them for application to American government and, in particular, Congress.

There, members sworn to govern in the interest of all the people have abdicated this responsibility in favor of intramural struggles for partisan sway. Republicans are—at the moment—in the forefront of this dereliction. Demographic and attitudinal tides in the country are turning against them. They've tried to delay the arrival of the future by turning the Republican Party into a labor union for the well-to-do.

Prominent in their strategy has been a fevered campaign against the president's new health-care program. This opposition is manifestly nourished by fear that the program will work and will thus create a grateful larger constituency for Democratic policies. Republicans in Congress first tried to keep people who needed the program from having it. Then they and allies have tried to dissuade people from using it. Party has mattered more than public needs.

In the larger scheme, if free-market nostrums from the political right can be come-ons to the credulous, nostrums from the left can be as well. To borrow phrases, they may invite crude and naïve trust in the goodness of those wielding political power and in the sacralized dogma of government as problem-solver. Even as our leaders differ on policy they are, at their worst, united on one point. They are Tweedledum and Tweedledee in wanting voters to think in bumper stickers and toe the party line. Political careerists benefit from this approach. The public does not.

In some of his thinking, Pope Francis has an unlikely bedfellow—the late anthropologist and writer Loren Eiseley. Though his writing was not religious, Eiseley was keenly attuned to the concept of a natural order. He thought we humans have learned to change it faster than we have learned to understand the consequences of changing it. He saw us becoming people who believe—naïvely—that everything worth knowing or having can be defined by technology and consumer economics. He had a term for this latest form of evolved Homo sapiens: Asphalt Man.

The Pope used different language for similar concerns. Here is what he said about material advances not matched by human advances: "...Epochal change has been set in motion by the enormous qualitative, quantitative rapid and cumulative advances occurring in the sciences and in technology, and by their instant application in different areas of nature and life. We are in an age of knowledge and information, which has led to new and often anonymous kinds of power."

To my ear, Pope Francis is concerned that robots and rocket ships could become our golden calf.

He is manifestly concerned about the state of the Roman Catholic Church. A discussion of the many good reasons for this would require more time and space than are here available. Perhaps useful evidence can be seen in reactions to the Pope's treatise. Conservative elements of his church grumbled that he did not tread heavily enough on their favorite issues of abortion and the like. (They were joined by presumptuous voices on the American political right.) Institutional norms were challenged, and the challenge was not welcomed.

Meanwhile, some of us feast in life while others starve. Rich men have tried to buy the presidency for one of their own, and they promise to try again. Congress has brought itself into public disgrace. And the Pope has become controversial by proclaiming an ethic of love and service.

Like fish perceiving water, we cannot be certain where we are on that rising and falling curve of human progress. But we can guess. Mine is that when history makes a list of societies whose value systems could have been better, we will be on it.

HOW REPUBLICANS SAY AMEN
MARCH 2, 2014

I had a letter the other day from my Uncle Barlow, who lives way out in the countryside in Barlow County. He wants my advice about a new challenge. Here's what he had to say.

Dear Nephew,

I've got this new situation to deal with, and I'd be mighty curious to have your opinion about how it's going.

You see, my Cousin Mavis has asked me to spend some time with her son Orlo. She's been raising the boy by herself ever since her husband Mandrell went missing. (The Widow Cumbee says he ran off with a podiatrist's wife from over at Tabor City, but we don't actually know if that's so, and anyhow it never has seemed to trouble Mavis much, so we just leave it alone.)

Mavis thinks the boy has got to an age where he needs a man's advice. She asked me to help out. I said sure, thinking I'd be talking to him about bullies and girls and such. But this boy has got a whole different kind of thing on his mind. You see, he's been following the news, and he's got some questions.

Well, over he came the other day, and we set up on the porch with some RC Cola and pork rinds, and he started right in. He wanted to record the whole thing for school, and I've sent along this copy so you can hear it for yourself.

Here's what the recording said.

ORLO: Well, Cousin Barlow, looks like the politicians are getting kind of wound up.

BARLOW: Yes, they truly are. There's some elections coming up, and they are maneuvering to get ready.

ORLO: Looks like those Republicans are getting extra restless. And what exactly is a Republican, anyway?

BARLOW: Well, son, even the Republicans aren't necessarily sure about that one nowadays, but if I had to try to put it in a nutshell I'd say a Republican is somebody who thinks the government shouldn't be too big and should leave people alone as much as it can.

ORLO: They think the government should pretty much try to leave people alone?

BARLOW: Yes, pretty much.

ORLO: Then why do they want to have all these rules to make women have babies?"

BARLOW: Well, son, you'll begin to learn as you grow up that sometimes people say one thing but do another.

ORLO: Oh, I see. Like those folks that flock down to the First Barlow County Church every Sunday.

BARLOW: Now you'll want to be careful about that. Religion and politics are two different things.

ORLO: Do those Republicans know that? They sure do seem to be friendly with a lot of those preachers. But I guess that does kind of make sense, seeing as how they are in similar lines of work.

BARLOW: Pardon?

ORLO: They both want to tell you what to do, and they both want you to send 'em money.

BARLOW: Yes, I do guess you could say that.

ORLO: Do those preachers tell their people who to vote for?

BARLOW: Not in so many words, no. But they are pretty slick about letting it be known what kind of politics they favor.

ORLO: Well, then, do their friends the politicians tell people to go to church?

BARLOW: No. Not in so many words.

ORLO: But what would happen if the politicians started favoring things the preachers didn't like?

BARLOW: Then I guess the preachers would stop leaning their way.

ORLO: So, to keep the deal going, the politicians have to favor the government doing things the preachers like?

BARLOW: Yes, I suppose so.

ORLO: Like those rules to make women have babies? That's kind of a big thing with some of those preachers, isn't it?

BARLOW: Well, that's for sure.

ORLO: So, the politicians don't tell people they have to go to church, but they do tell people they have to do what the preachers want 'em to do.

BARLOW: Uh, huh.

ORLO: Is that why some of the politicians want to make rules against gay people, too? Because of what the preachers say?

BARLOW: That's certainly mixed up in it, yes.

ORLO: Is it contagious? Can you catch it?

BARLOW: Is what contagious, son?

ORLO: Gay-ness. Being gay. Some of those people act like they're afraid if we let gay people have the same rules as everybody else, then everybody would want to be gay.

BARLOW: No, son. Being gay is not contagious.

ORLO: Then why are those preachers and their friends so hot against it?

BARLOW: They say it goes against the Bible.

ORLO: Oh, my goodness. Did Jesus say it's bad to be gay?

BARLOW: No, Jesus didn't mention it one way or the other. The folks who talk about it being against the Bible are talking about the Old Testament.

ORLO: Isn't that the part of the Bible that talks about not eating shellfish and such?

BARLOW: Yes, that's it.

ORLO: If a lot of those Republicans get elected, will I have to give up shrimp?

BARLOW: No, son. The preachers and their friends skip those parts. The Bible is a very long book, and it has a lot of different parts to it.

ORLO: So, they kind of pick and choose the parts they want to get hot about?

BARLOW: Yes, pretty much.

ORLO: But suppose I read the Bible, and I favor different parts of it than they do?

BARLOW: I guess they wouldn't like that.

ORLO: So these preachers want their politician friends to make government rules about what kind of religion people have to favor?

BARLOW: It does kind of amount to that, yes.

ORLO: And about sex, and who's got to have babies, and stuff like that?

BARLOW: Among other things, yes.

ORLO: Well, all I can say is, thank goodness.

BARLOW: Pardon?

ORLO: Thank goodness those Republicans say the government should try to leave people alone. Heaven knows what they'd be doing if they said the government ought to get all up in our personal and private business.

That's where Uncle Barlow's recording ended. He went on in his letter to say that he isn't sure what kind of advice to give young Orlo, and to ask my opinion.

I will drop Uncle Barlow a line and tell him I think Orlo has a pretty good handle on things all by himself.

LIES, DAMN LIES, AND
REPUBLICANS
APRIL 2, 2014

There ain't nothin' more powerful than the
odor of mendacity.

—Big Daddy Pollitt in *Cat on a Hot Tin Roof*

Time was, politicians might fear being caught in a lie. If Big Daddy were to sniff the air today, he would surely say that times have changed.

Lies are so common in political discourse that news outlets devote continuing features to enumerating and explaining them. At the moment, Republicans would win a contest scored on frequency and gall. They are struggling with obsolescence in their brand, and with an acute anemia of leadership.

Their presidential crop may be even thinner than in 2012, when their ticket featured a clueless plutocrat and a partisan hustler. Now, in the echo chambers of their early season speechfests, a darling has been Sen. Rand Paul, son of former Rep. Ron Paul—a pair whose behavior suggests the existence of a crackpot gene. Sen. Marco Rubio's name appears occasionally on the marquee. But it flickers. The young senator is noticeably green, and his voter appeal could be debated: he gained his Senate seat by winning a multicandidate election in which more people voted for someone else than for him.

New Jersey Gov. Chris Christie is struggling awkwardly to rise above scandal. He claims that when his staff took it upon themselves to lock the door to New York City, he just didn't notice. Meanwhile, confirming that he is not a natural for the china shop of diplomacy, he startled an influential Jewish audience with references to Israeli "occupied territories."

Christie confuses swaggering with leadership, or he hopes voters will. And with magnified scrutiny, he may begin to resemble Boss Tweed in more than girth. Mindful of this, old-guard Republicans are trying to gin up enthusiasm for still another member of the Bush family, former Florida governor Jeb Bush. Among those displaying markedly restrained enthusiasm is Jeb Bush himself.

The weakness of the Republican brand is profound, and not only as it was symbolized in Mitt Romney's royalist view of government. Demographic shifts and evolving attitudes are moving the country away from ideas the GOP insists on standing for.

In extremis, the party has resorted to chicanery. This has sustained mindless, showboat attacks on a duly elected president. In Congress it has produced dangerous obstruction. At the state level, it has produced laws nakedly intended to impede voting by likely Democrats.

And it is about to fuel fanciful claims that superior policy positions are moving Republicans toward gains in off-year Congressional elections.

The truth is twofold:

- Republicans will gain Congressional seats in the November elections.
- The districts up for decision this year are so heavily gerrymandered that a fire hydrant could win on the Republican ticket.

Time is against the Republican Party as it now stands, both the old barons and the Tea Party faction that is clutching them in a death dance. Time is also against cranks, opportunists, and vigilantes in public life. The American electorate—patient to a fault in the aggregate—eventually insists that leaders pay effective attention to the glamourless, sleeves-up business of running the country.

For now we are left to regret that a major political party has passed into the hands of people who display little respect for the citizens they supposedly represent and little regard for integrity in the democratic process.

Thus an irony emerges for people who know that thoughtful conservatism makes a useful contribution to political discourse: their best hope may be that today's Republican Party will finally shake itself apart and leave room for better.

MY SECRET SHAME
MAY 27, 2014

I n the spring, when others' fancies turn to rebirth and renewal, mine turn to introspection and self-discipline. I belong to
a tribe of men who share a serious existential problem. Mother
Nature doesn't like us. Not one bit.

I have learned this cosmic truth in a succession of suburban
yards. My first, years ago, had been owned by a retired couple with
a passion for flower gardening. Friends asked me gingerly if I—a
neophyte—really meant to tackle the care of it on my own. With
grand assurance I told them I did indeed.

Foolish me. Mother Nature quickly brought me to heel. Shrubs
that had thrived for years sickened when my shadow fell across
them. Hardy leaves grew odd tumors. Blossoms wilted mysteriously
overnight. My visits for advice at nurseries occasioned impromptu
staff meetings and murmurs of puzzled amazement.

Over the years I've had similar luck with lawns. They defy my
every effort. If one corner thrives, another withers. I have been

host to the United Nations of weeds. My yard care has had the single virtue of consistency. Through many years and five states, I have replicated one result. Picture corn stubble.

We outcasts of Mother Nature are a tribe of secret shame. We recognize each other by the look in our eyes; however, our shame has nothing to do with a sense of failure. We are perfectly happy for our egos to shelter in the mastery of some other skill—in a facility for card games, say, or a way with hammers and saws; in a knack with dogs or a flair in the kitchen. In these modern times, the definition of manliness has acquired enough scope to offer us a variety of havens.

No, our shame is of a moral sort. Our affliction causes us to resent perfectly decent people.

A man who lived near one of my homes was both a neighbor and a friend. A fine fellow all around. Good company and a solid citizen. We shared drinks and fun and serious conversation, too. I was glad to know him.

And I lived in fear of his discovering that I ground my teeth whenever I looked in the direction of his house and yard. They were a portrait of perfection. The grass was a carpet. The trees were manicured. He maintained this Eden with scarcely any effort. In the spring, he sprinkled a little of this and that. His plants prospered. In the fall, when he blew away leaves, they stayed where he put them. Every one. Year-round, he achieved in minutes what I labored at for hours without a scrap of proper result. I cherished my friend in fellowship but hated him for his yard.

Another friend in another town had only to gesture, and Mother Nature danced. He grew his own herbs. His tomatoes thrived. The first time I tried to grow tomatoes, the family dog plucked them from the vine at secret times of her own mysterious devising. I contrived to have this friend visit my house more often than I visited his. He never seemed to notice the manipulation.

Nonetheless, we humans are a hopeful lot. We endure; and sometimes, through endurance, we prevail. At length I decided that I need not be forever exiled from harmony with the natural world. I would feed birds. As this involved no expectation that seeds would actually germinate, it seemed a reasonable undertaking.

I had not reckoned on squirrels. They were so many and so hungry that the cost of birdseed became a noticeable item in my monthly budget. They devised acrobatic means of defeating squirrel-proof feeders. They did pause briefly when I laced the birdseed with cayenne pepper. Then they learned to like it. They could have been tasters at a Cajun cooking contest.

Squirrels still harass me, and I still harass them. Awhile back, in a naïve spasm, I planted pansies. The squirrels ate the blossoms. I now possess an arsenal of chemical repellents. All natural, the labels tell me. All vile, my nose tells me. The squirrels watch until I forget to spray. Then they dine.

Ours is a relationship of sorts, even with its overtones of guerrilla warfare. I persist because it just doesn't seem right for a man to be totally excluded from involvement with the natural world. It doesn't seem…well, natural for all the territory beyond my window panes to be a foreign land.

In every other regard, my life skills are simple but solid. I do a good job of cleaning a bathroom. I can tell a decent joke. Small children seem to like me.

And I have learned, I believe, to carry with grace the burden of my guilt. To soldier on. I can smile serenely through the longest discussion of horticultural success. Others do not glimpse my inner struggle. I am a rock.

In fact, there is a man in my neighborhood who has a perfect yard. He is also a friend, and…

Oh, well.

WASHINGTON:
ATTACK OF THE MICROBES
JULY 3, 2014

*Everything is changing. People are taking their comedians
seriously and the politicians as a joke.*

—Will Rogers

When Joseph Medill was publisher of the *Chicago Tribune* in
the late nineteenth century, the newspaper closely reflected his views. Medill's views were not well informed on some matters. Science was among these.

For a time he was fascinated by sunspots. And in the pages
of the *Tribune*, as a matter of policy, all natural phenomena were
attributed to sunspots. Abruptly, Medill became interested in

microbes. And abruptly, in the pages of the Tribune, sunspots disappeared. All natural phenomena were thenceforth attributed to microbes.

It might be a stretch to call today's politics natural phenomena. But in explanation of them, microbes and sunspots make about as much sense as anything.

Consider Vice-President Joe Biden and former Secretary of State Hillary Clinton. In them, we lately have two of the most powerful people in the world pleading penury.

Biden is known to be a wag; however, he did not appear to be in joking mode here. And he amplified his claim with particulars that were demonstrably—let us try to put this as charitably as possible—not consistent with fact. Sometimes Ol' Joe's gaffes are only that. He's been called the kind of guy who'd bring a ham sandwich to a Seder meal. Maybe this was just one of those times when he talked faster than he thought.

Clinton's comic muse has long since decamped. The possibility of levity need not be considered in her case. So, what the dickens was she up to? She knocks down a six-figure fee for making a speech. Husband Bill's net worth is estimated in the tens of millions.

Sometimes, when we desperately want to be liked, we blurt things we regret. It can happen to anyone. By all accounts she must be powerfully regretting this one.

On other fronts:

- Sen. Ted Cruz, the Texas vigilante, strikes poses suggesting he is available for a presidential nod. The notion of a Cruz presidency is credible to people who think a diverse electorate could be led by a man who is genuinely offended by differences of opinion.

Congress continues its serial homage to the Keystone Kops.

- Speaker of the House John Boehner continues hoping that his ranting will camouflage his bumbling.
- The Supreme Court has opened still another channel for fat-cat political money. Chief Justice John Roberts decorated this ruling with a pronouncement that large contributions by wealthy individuals do not necessarily create a presumption that wealthy individuals will exercise extra influence. Television comedian Bill Maher said this opinion could have been written by the "Little Mermaid." Sounds about right.
- The Supreme Court has ruled that businesses can have religion and are allowed to enforce it upon their employees. Memo to the Little Mermaid: Maybe you want to reconsider your desire to become human.
- New Jersey Gov. Chris Christie has tried to preserve his bona fides by claiming that when his staff locked the door to New York City, he, gosh, just didn't notice. He remains presidential timber because he is such a stand-up guy. We could give him the keys to the Pentagon and rest easy. He would pay attention next time. Honest.
- Like tedious relatives who simply won't go home, an assortment of yesterday's crackpots and has-beens...well, simply won't go home.

As we see no witch crushed beneath a fallen house, we must conclude that Auntie Em is not on her way to wake us from an outlandish dream. All this really is happening.

About the Supreme Court, we can only sigh and wait. Not for the first time it has been peppered with appointees better known for ideology than for ability. The court has seen a resurgence of competence before, and eventually it will again.

Of political discourse we must say there's not much of the genuine article nowadays. Neither does Hillary Clinton's performance so far offer improvement. In her silly claims of financial struggle, and in her response to the hoots that followed, she has been notably tone deaf. In interviews she can pirouette through an answer without honestly touching on the substance of the question asked. And she regularly does.

Our public life is crowded with figures who seem less interested in messages that will resonate than in messages that are easy to swallow. It is as if they have so long urged us to think in the idiom of bumper stickers that they've begun doing so themselves. Or they use sloganeering to costume mere ambition. Or they resort to it because they genuinely don't know what to say to the public in these complex times.

Seen through the knothole of the 2016 presidential election, our next few years may be an era of conspicuously weak leadership. Hopeful hearts have wanted Hillary Clinton to be an exception. But so far she doesn't reliably stand out from the crowd.

GOD LOVE DARWIN
SEPTEMBER 19, 2014

E ndlessly we debate: Darwin or the Bible? And endlessly the debate is full of caricature. The Bible is freighted with claims it does not make. Hearsay versions of 150-year-old science are proclaimed as if they were holy writ. Fact goes wanting.

An open and literate society ought to do better.

For starters, the theory of natural selection was never seamless. With Newton and other pioneers, Charles Darwin explained much but not all in his field of inquiry. He himself noted the failure of some phenomena to fit where his grid said they ought.

Critiques, caveats, and elaborations from other scientists soon followed publication of *The Origin of Species* in 1859. They have followed plentifully ever since. Today's evolutionary thinking is far more varied than Darwin's. And around it even yet remain puzzles, anomalies, and disagreements.

The biblical side of the debate is compromised by America's culture of scriptural ignorance. The constitutional idea of church-state separation has spread widely into aspects of thought and attitude it was never meant to govern. In our popular mindset, freedom of religion has morphed into freedom from religion.

Even among observant Americans, the Bible is far more often cited than actually read. It may never be directly encountered in the completion of a so-called liberal education. Ostensibly literate people may be little aware of its broad impact on Western culture.

And what a pity for them to miss, say, the grandeur of Job:

Then the Lord answered Job out of the whirlwind:
"Who is this that darkens counsel by words without knowledge?
"Gird up your loins like a man. I will question you, and you shall declare to me.
"Where were you when I laid the foundations of the Earth?
"Tell me, if you have understanding.
"Who determined its measurements—surely you know!
"Or who stretched the line upon it?
"On what were its bases sunk, or who laid its cornerstone when the morning stars sang together and all the heavenly beings shouted for joy?
"Or who shut the sea in with doors when it burst out from the womb?
"When I made the clouds its garment and thick darkness its swaddling band
"And prescribed bounds for it, and set bars and doors
"And said, 'This far shall you come and no farther, and here shall your proud waves be stopped?'
"Have you commanded the morning since your days began,
"And caused the dawn to know its place,
"So that it might take hold of the skirts of the Earth
"And the wicked be shaken out of it?"

Or how about Paul at his best?

> If I speak in the tongues of mortals and of angels but do not
> have love, I am a noisy gong or a clanging cymbal. And if
> I have prophetic powers and understand all mysteries and
> all knowledge, and if I have all faith, so as to remove moun-
> tains, but do not have love, I am nothing. If I give away all
> my possessions, and if I hand over my body so that I may
> boast, but do not have love, I gain nothing.
>
> Love is patient, love is kind; love is not envious or boastful
> or arrogant or rude. It does not insist on its own way; it is
> not irritable or resentful; it does not rejoice in wrongdo-
> ing but rejoices in the truth. It bears all things, believes all
> things, hopes all things, endures all things.
>
> Love never ends...

A greater pity is this: The Bible's confinement at the outskirts of
cultural literacy makes Americans sitting ducks for quackery, chicanery, and foolishness—for televangelist hucksters, for opportunists with a taste for political influence, and for all sorts of glib
nonsense about what the Bible is and about what it actually says.

Take, for example, the idea of measuring the Bible by the standards of a modern history book—a model that cannot be sensibly
applied if only because the form was unknown at the time of the
biblical writings.

In this light, what of Genesis?

It is nearer to being a sermon or, more precisely, a conflation
of sermons. Also, it is a treasury of artful communication. Imagine
being a writer-editor working in the context of an ancient and marginally literate theocracy. Imagine wanting to articulate the idea
that humans had broken with God by arrogating to themselves the

definition of good and evil. Toward this end, the image of stealing fruit from the tree of knowledge is marvelously effective.

And where outside of Genesis do seven words better capture a descent from innocence into worldly shame: "Who told you that you were naked?"

Or consider the example of Jonah. If we are to take the Bible seriously, must we believe that a big fish literally swallowed a man whole and then spit him out, alive, days later?

The question is without worthwhile point.

In the story, God tells Jonah to take His word to Nineveh, where a great deal of sinning has been going on. Jonah feels the people of Nineveh don't deserve that kind of attention. He tries to run away and, in the process, lands in the belly of the fish.

Three days and three nights later, he is back on dry land, hearing again the divine command to go and preach in Nineveh. Reluctantly, Jonah complies. He admonishes the Ninevites to repent—and in a trice, they all do. God sees their repentance and forgives them.

Jonah's reaction? He is sullen and resentful. He thinks the Almighty should have handed out more justice and less mercy. As the brief story ends, God leaves a still-sulking Jonah to ponder its real point: why should God not cherish all his creatures?

Understood in the context of its time, place, and culture, this is a teaching story—and a good one. It is about obedience and the abundance of divine love. The business about the fish is peripheral to the spirit and the purpose of the tale.

Even so, we moderns say, we are moderns, after all. What might be something nearer to our own experience?

Examples of teaching stories abound in our literature. I think of Harper Lee's classic novel, *To Kill a Mockingbird*. It is a story about values and about the potentially high cost of being faithful to them. The human issues it portrays are quite real. The lessons it advances are quite real. Worrying about the historicity of Atticus

Finch would be as useful as worrying that Lewis Carroll might never actually have seen a Bandersnatch.

The Bible is a wonderfully diverse and sophisticated collection of books, poems, songs, letters, and other forms of literature not seen today. It is a record across centuries of how individuals, groups, and whole cultures have lived out their need to express their experience of God.

And nothing in it requires us to suppose that God could not have chosen evolutionary tools to bring the human race to the forefront of His creation. There is no necessary conflict between science and faith.

But American culture has traveled to an ironic extreme. Reverence is reserved for technology, while religious faith is elbowed out of sight. Nowadays you may be deemed merely colorful if, in polite conversation, you tell a naughty story or drop an expletive. But venture aloud a serious mention of God, and you may be charged with a true breach of manners.

Yes, prudent minimums of courtesy do recommend that we refrain from pushing values on each other willy-nilly. But when did we decide that Americans must be guaranteed of living beyond sight or sound of any manifestation of faith?

And where did we lose the intellectual rigor to recognize that our culture has rigged the discussion of faith and reason?

C. S. Lewis is helpful on this point. He wrote of being in a dark toolshed on a bright afternoon. A shaft of sunlight angled through a crack above the door. From a position to one side, he could see the sunbeam, the motes drifting in it, and the objects it fell upon. Standing in the sunbeam and looking upward along it, he could see nothing inside the shed, only a framed view of leaves, branches, and the sky beyond.

We would quickly demur if someone claimed that one of these perspectives was inherently more "real" than the other, that one was objective in ways that the other was not. So, too, we must demur from suggestions that the engagement of faithful people in the "real world" is not "impartial," that it is compromised ipso facto by their very faith.

Yet our culture makes the claim nonetheless, and it even hijacks the definition of terms. Faith is characterized as chosen belief, in the way that one might choose to accept the word of a trusted friend. Our cultural vocabulary does not credit the possibility of faith being an objectively real experience—as can the experience of beauty, in a very pale analogy.

Our idiom does not bother to assail the proposition but simply ignores it. This mode of thinking is not rationalism or even skepticism. It is intellectual dishonesty in expedient disguise. But it does simplify discussion by evading the essential questions.

An open and literate society ought to do better.

UNCLE BARLOW MEETS DULCINEA AND MITCH MCCONNELL NOVEMBER 11, 2014

I got another letter from my Uncle Barlow the other day. He still lives way out in the country, in Barlow County. He thinks that because I live in the city, I have more experience with certain kinds of things, so now and then he writes me to ask for my opinion.

Lately he's been thinking about culture and politics. Here's what he had to say.

Dear Nephew,

Well, I just came back from spending the morning with Scooter over at the café, and I want to tell you, he's down in the dumps in the worst way. You see, his wife Ida has got it in her head that she needs to be more cultured. She has been after him to take her up to Charlotte to see the symphony, and he figured she wasn't going to let it go, so last week up they went.

Scooter said the music was mighty pretty, but he just couldn't figure out the method of the thing. He said a fellow in a funeral suit stood in front of the musicians and waved a little stick at them, even though they weren't looking at him, since they had to keep their eyes on the music they were playing. He said the only thing he could dope out was that the fellow must have been some kind of big wheel and they had to let him get up there with the rest of the bunch if he wanted to. Kind of like when we were boys and Booger Braxton owned the football so we always had to let him play quarterback.

But anyhow, that's not what Scooter is down in the dumps about. On the way home in the car Ida started going on about how she didn't like having such a plain name, and she was thinking about starting to call herself Dulcinea. Scooter said he checked around, and that's a name from a story about a fellow who rides around trying to stick a spear in a windmill. So now Scooter is afraid that Ida's butter is beginning to slip off her noodle. He doesn't quite know what to do. He's saying that he read something not long ago about recreational therapy and maybe he will try to get her interested in football.

Ordinarily I would have stopped by the library on the way home, but I skipped this time because it's kind of tense over there nowadays. Millie the librarian got mighty cranky when all those Republicans won in the election. Millie would sooner kiss a snake than smile at a Republican.

Well, who should come into the library the very next day but Orlo Babcock? He owns the tractor dealership out on the bypass. I guess Orlo got to going on about how the Republicans are going to fix things so the free enterprise system prevails and folks are only rewarded for working hard on their own initiative to get ahead. And I guess Millie said she thought he and his kind are mighty free about recommending bootstraps to people who don't have any boots to begin with. And then he called her a woolly minded liberal do-gooder, and she got to stabbing him in the chest with her finger and calling him a buffoon, which is a touchy thing to say to Orlo Babcock, because it's true. Well, Orlo used to be on the library board and still has friends there, and Millie is stalking around saying she won't be bullied, and I'm thinking to steer clear of there until things settle down.

Now, ordinarily I don't spend much time studying on politicians. I figure those folks are a lot more interested in each other than they are in me. As long as they don't raise the taxes on my land or my liquor I figure I'm pretty much OK. But I have to admit this election does have me puzzled about a couple of things. The first thing is, how did all those Republicans get elected? I mean, near as I can tell, they didn't say much of anything except that they really didn't like President Obama, who's not going to be around much longer in any case.

It kind of put me in mind of when that fellow Nixon was running for president and said he had a plan for ending the Vietnam War, but it had to be a secret, but he wanted people to vote for it anyway. Well of course he went right on and got elected, which proved I guess that voters sometimes will actually buy a pig in a poke, and now by golly it looks like they've done it again.

So, come the new Congress in a little while, the Senate Republicans are going to be led by this fellow Mitch McConnell from Kentucky. You can recognize him right away if you see his picture in the paper. He's the one who looks kind of like he's not all there. He says he and his bunch are going to end the gridlock in Washington, which may be pretty brassy of him to brag about, since I hear he was one of the leaders causing it in the first place. It's kind of like somebody asking you to admire them for agreeing to stop hitting you in the head.

And that brings me to the rest of what I'm wondering, which is, now that those Republicans are in control, what are they actually going to do about things? They can't go on just giving President Obama the dickens. Well, I guess they could, but I mean they've already made it plain they think he's worse than your ex-wife's second husband. What's the point? And what does that have to do with the work they are supposed to get on with themselves?

The Widow Cumbee says I should try to look at things in a positive way. She says we should all try to see it kind of like we'd been given a mystery gift for Christmas. But I can't get very far with that, because I'm kind of nervous that maybe the people who got together to give us the gift don't know what's in the box, either, but we're all going to have to live with whatever pops out.

The Widow Cumbee says I'm just a worrywart. I sure would like to know what you think about all this, nephew. And in the meantime I hope you keep well.

Sincerely,

Your Uncle Barlow.

THUGS R US
DECEMBER 15, 2014

One afternoon many years ago, I had played hooky from work to catch the latest action movie. Only a few people were in the theater—all slackers like me, I assumed.

At a climactic moment, the hero had an especially vile bad guy in the sights of an enormous handgun. With a squint and a growl, the good guy delivered his signature line: "Do ya feel lucky, punk? Well, do ya?"

In one of the theater's forward rows, a man leaped to his feet and pumped his fists in the air. "Shoot the bastard!" he shouted. "Kill him! Kill him! Kill him!"

In the years since, I've thought of that episode when listening to rounds of a perennial debate: Do our attitudes shape our entertainment, or vice versa? Did the movie inflame my fellow slacker? Or did the movie-makers have him in mind when they framed their offering for an audience?

I've thought about that episode in connection with pornography. I've thought about it in connection with the dreadful lows of reality television. And I've thought about it lately in the uproar over incidents of domestic violence among professional football players.

If we consider only the statistics of the football thing, the incidents were few and isolated. So, what explains a wave of reaction that has reached all the way to Congress? I think the explanation is this: Professional football is a haven for thugs, and the fact is widely known. Thugs do not typify the men who play professional football. But they are plentiful enough, and they are protected.

An appetite for games is elemental in human nature. Children learn through play. Adults are restored by it. The late journalist and social commentator Walter Kerr argued that the word "recreation" means precisely what its component parts say: RE-CREATION.

An instinct for sporting competition also is human. We are naturally curious to know whose eye is keener, whose horse faster, whose arm stronger. Communally organized sporting competition comes down to us from antiquity. The scope of it would appear to grow in direct proportion to the availability of disposable time and money. Thus the extremes of organized sport in today's America demonstrate the levels of extravagance that a fabulously wealthy society is able and willing to support.

The barons of professional football—the team owners—are selling two commodities. One is entertainment in the form of performance by superior athletes. And a fine athletic performance is gratifying to watch. It reminds us that the human body and brain working together are capable of performing marvels. Competitive sports can indeed have something to say to us about human skill, teamwork, perseverance, even courage.

The owners' second commodity for sale is victory. And this, I think, is the party drug that begins to cloud our judgment. We feel the better competitor should win, yes. We feel that winning is a token of merit, yes. This much is part of us as humans. But professional athletes who consistently win make more money. They enjoy more fame. And so, some of them begin to value winning even by means that have nothing to do with athletic skill. They resort to violence and intimidation. The ethic goes beyond winning the game toward beating—in the full sense of the term—the opponent. Some players try to stack the deck of competition by injuring key players on the other side. The end not only justifies the means, it pays handsomely. And it pays those closely associated with the winner as well.

We all know this. We know that the sleek young wife beater in the pricey wardrobe is cruising through life on money that a great many of us have been ever so glad to pay him. Thus I think that the surge of reaction to recent events rises from the fact that in our heart of hearts, we are not surprised. We are not surprised that men who display an aptitude for fan-financed violence display a taste for personal violence as well.

As a dilettante follower of professional football, I am culpable, too. And I was, after all, in that theater years ago to see a movie whose character I knew full well when I walked in. If I was not on my feet shouting murder, I do remember thinking that the punk deserved whatever he got.

Thus we have professional football in twenty-first-century America: human nature undergirded by societal wealth so lavish that average men and women can afford to spend thousands in pursuit of a game. The owners' cartel—the National Football League—now announces that it will develop stronger rules about off-the-field behavior. With wetted finger aloft, the owners' kept regulators will weasel toward "reforms" until the wind of public opinion no longer offers to reach damaging strength.

Clearly we do not feel, in the aggregate, that all of this amounts to mortal sin. If we did, presumably we would change our ways. But it is a shabby thing. And surely the lords of the sport could better refrain from riding their privilege to the very outskirts of decent limits.

THE CUSTOMER IS ALWAYS RIPE
FEBRUARY 4, 2015

I have never seen an airline employee use a cattle prod on passengers. However, the image does occur to me, and not only when I travel. To my mind it symbolizes the fading of a venerable term—customer service—toward that nether region where outmoded concepts go to be quaint. There it will join smaller casualties of changing times, such as the personal letter. And it will join much greater ones, such as two from the world of politics, dignity and tolerance.

Of course airlines are not alone in treating customers as a necessary evil. The style has been favored for years by insurance companies, which are keen to sell their product but loath to see it actually used.

Yet who would have foreseen a day when many businesses deal with customers by resourcefully hiding from them? We've all had the experience. The automated phone tree offers me every option for service except the one I really need. The automated, online help page, with its list of Frequently Asked Questions, suggests that I am the only person on the planet who wants to know what I want to know. My question is not frequently asked. It is not even occasionally asked. I am an outlier on the bell curve of customer behavior. I am a nuisance.

In the uncommon event that these robots clearly offer the option of access to a human being, the human being is too busy to talk right away, even though my call is Very Important to Us. The human being is helping other customers—most of whom, like me, are twiddling their thumbs on hold. Our time, in the aggregate, is less important than the time of the human being whose wages we are paying and who supposedly is employed for our convenience.

As the country learned the hard way, the ethic of customers-as-chattel has penetrated the banking industry as well. And it has seeped all the way down to affect the smallest of the small fry, people like me.

My requirements of my bank are simple. I want my money safely kept. I want portions of it promptly returned to me when I ask. But nowadays, to gain access to my own money, I must run a gauntlet of sales pitches:

> Teller: "Have you considered our new warp-speed account bundle with color-coded deposit and withdrawal slips?"
> Me: "Yes. I've heard about it. But I don't want it, thank you."
> Teller: "But you're missing so much."
> Me: "I'm aware of what I'm missing. I don't need it."
> Teller: "But you could have funds automatically moved among your accounts at night, and receive a complete update on your cellphone the next morning."
> Me: "I don't need to bank while I sleep, and I don't want to do arithmetic before breakfast."
> Teller, eyebrows arching: "Really!"

I am old enough to remember when banks offered toasters as sales inducements. Now they offer scolding and guilt.

In his satirical comic strip "Li'l Abner," the late Al Capp presented the character of the shmoo. A shmoo was a chubby little bowling pin of a creature with a cheerful grin and a bottomless desire to enhance the happiness of human beings.

Shmoos were plentiful. They reproduced exponentially and asexually. They needed only air. They abundantly gave eggs, milk, and butter (no churning needed). And shmoos gave themselves. If a shmoo sensed that a nearby human being was hungry, it would cheerfully cook itself for dinner. Fried shmoo tasted like chicken. Broiled shmoo tasted like steak. Shmoos would undergo any circumstance to please.

At the epicenter of commerce by shakedown—industries with monopolistic advantage—there is a certain inescapable shmooness in the customer role. Other industries may be thinking wishfully when they adopt the model. I know of businesses that will not hand me over to an automaton when I need service. I favor them vigorously when I shop, and I am not alone in this.

We probably should not imagine a focused consumer revolt. But traditional business may not be immune to the kind of creeping customer desertion that mortally wounded the American auto industry and American newspapers.

Meanwhile, at certain points of my consumer need, I suppose I must grin shmoo-like and learn to live with realities.

A bank is, whatever else, a better repository than a mattress. Usually.

HIDE! THE HOMOS ARE COMING
FEBRUARY 13, 2015

During the Depression era, a friend of mine lived in the deepest, most poverty-ravaged parts of the South. Options in public policy were grim, problems intractable. Better tomorrows were a melancholy dream. The tenure of public officeholders was likely to be marked by a stringent shortage of results for the electorate. Politicians had to sell something other than accomplishment.

One politician in my friend's home state cruised regularly to election and reelection. In political season, when he went out on the stump, he stationed henchmen in the audiences of his speeches. Early in his delivery, on cue, they would begin shouting, "Tell us about the niggers. Tell us about the niggers." With gusto he did, thus evading forthright treatment of his constituents' dismal lot and his own meager record. He was the people's champion against scapegoats of his own expedient choosing.

I recalled this story of political hatemongering when I read that presidential hopefuls Mike Huckabee and Rand Paul will appear in a new antigay film. It is being called—without discernible irony—a documentary. It portrays the advancement of gay marriage as a threat to the Christian faith. "If homosexual activists get everything they want, it will be nothing less than the criminalization of Christianity," one figure argues in the film.

The looming presidential season has already offered other excursions into the twilight zone. Senator Paul is a regular tour leader. Just recently, within the space of a week, he took opposite positions on the issue of childhood vaccination. He continues to lie about his education credentials, despite having been caught in it years ago. He is a human gaffe-fest. As the son of perennial gadfly Ron Paul, he poses a question for science: could crackpot bumbling be hereditary?

Meanwhile, New Jersey Gov. Chris Christie has taken a colorful show on the road. With choreographed outbursts of faux spontaneity, he touts poor self-control as a leadership skill. And lurking in the wings of the political stage are more than a dozen dreamers, has-beens, opportunists, and oddballs who are likelier to be canonized than elected to the White House. Their declarations of presidential aspiration suggest that some have noted the Sarah Palin model. Political celebrity can pay well. No electoral success required.

Huckabee may be one of the mercenary group. The ordained minister has diligently shaped himself into a brand, in the idiom of today's marketeers. As a candidate, television and radio personality, speaker-for-hire, and author, he has established himself in an aw-shucks vein of right-wing commentary on social and political issues. The title of his latest book conveys well enough the sizzle of product-Huckabee: *God, Guns, Grits, and Gravy.*

He cannot think that cornpone formulations will resonate with a varied national audience. Hence my suspicion that he aims to prosper in a niche market. He might be welcome to do this were his methods not base. He is, of course, far from being the first politician to demonize minorities. But as an observant Christian, I find his Bible-thumping version of it especially noxious. Permitting gay Americans to formalize loving relationships threatens nothing and harms no one.

Elsewhere in the presidential pose-a-thon: Wisconsin's bully-boy Gov. Scott Walker is shucking and jiving past the simplest questions. Florida's Jeb Bush is severing financial ties that might appear unseemly for a presidential aspirant—and are, in fact, unseemly for a presidential aspirant. Hillary Clinton is assembling a major campaign machine while purporting to be undecided about campaigning. Ditto Texas Sen. Ted Cruz, who salivates over power. Vice President Joe Biden is making a show of plucking petals off his inner decision-daisy. Wannabes of every sort are searching for a shtick.

Our national air reeks of politics whose aim is less to lead the people than to herd them. The election is not quite two years away. I fear it will seem a lot longer.

SAY HOWDY TO MENDACITY
MAY 13, 2015

I n the vintage Western movie *Hondo*—based on a story by the late novelist and poet Louis L'Amour—John Wayne protects a widow and her little boy from marauding Apaches. A key scene has the Apache war chief offering to release the three of them if Wayne will promise to conceal the Indians' whereabouts from approaching cavalry. In response, the Duke growls, "This I will not do." The chief smiles in affirmation of Wayne's refusal to be a traitor and lets them go anyway. The chief's proposition was a test, Wayne later explains to the widow: "Indians hate a liar."

Though pooh-poohed by the smart set, Wayne's westerns were not bad work. And they were about more than cowboys and Indians. This one was about integrity. The scene with the war chief was one of the theme-setters. The stereotype of the noble red man was used as counterpoint to white characters whose standards of behavior were not right and wrong but advantage and expediency. An Indian hated lies. Did "civilized" white men? Maybe, maybe not.

Even Louis L'Amour might deem his metaphors quaint in to-day's world. While most of us would say we dislike deceit, people who want our attention and allegiance plentifully bet that we are flexible on the point. If they weasel on matters of integrity, will we turn away from them? Maybe, maybe not.

Hillary Clinton would be high on this list. She has entered the presidential race carrying—as ever—baggage. She is said to be careless of appropriate boundaries between her public duty and her private interests. Details of the Clintons' alleged indiscretions may be perennially debatable; however, it seems fair to observe that the debate is, in fact, perennial. Also, we may usefully note the announced theme of her presidential campaign: She's an ordi-nary gal. Just one of the folks, like you and me. This theme has the virtue of being warm and the telltale defect of being manifestly untrue.

Meanwhile, over at NBC network news, anchor Brian Williams is half way through a six-month suspension for fibbing in some of his news reports. For this offense, a lesser light would have been fired before lunchtime. But Williams is a star. The audience likes him. He boosts ratings, and ratings boost revenue. NBC manage-ment holds open the possibility that Williams will return to the air. Commercial imperatives are being weighed. Will integrity weigh as much? Maybe, maybe not.

(Less of a stir has been caused by similar accusations against one of the stars in Fox News's cast of performers. My theory: The Fox faithful refuse to believe it, and no one else is surprised.)

If popular sports can reflect values in an affluent culture—and they can—the example of the New England Patriots' football team is worth considering. The Patriots have been caught cheating, and not for the first time. In this iteration, they deflated footballs for eas-ier handling in a key game. Early explanations scapegoated a couple of underlings, but speculation would not ignore an obvious point: golden-boy quarterback Tom Brady cannot have failed to know.

Brady smirked and baffle-gabbed his way past the question until an investigation concluded the obvious: he cannot have failed to know. The league suspended him for four games and fined the Patriots' organization $1 million.

As commercial entertainment, professional football can let its standards be a matter for vendors, customers, and the kept regulators who eventually get around to slapping wrists. But will fans ever fully forget that Brady is a cheat? Will they always wonder if victory involves a little performance-enhancing funny business with the rules? Integrity is a Humpty-Dumpty thing. In seeing the Patriots twice resolve to win by any means, and twice skate through being caught, football consumers have received notice: they are at risk of buying an adulterated product.

Corruption in journalism is, obviously, a more serious issue. But television news has one foot inextricably in show business. The telling thing in the NBC episode is less Brian Williams's deceit than the network's long pause in deciding how much it matters. Eventually, television may decide to reconsider the whole institution of the prime-time news anchor. Consumers with multiplying options for obtaining news and information could lose appetite for a standing appointment with a friendly face.

Among adulterated products, the Clinton candidacy should concern us sharply. Given her lead over Democrats, and the Keystone Kops nature of the Republican field, she is likelier than anyone now in view to be the next president. Yet she has bought into the ethic that political leadership consists of finding a marketable pose. We must hope she knows better and would eventually choose to do better.

ABOUT AN EMPTY MAN
JUNE 8, 2015

Once I knew a man who was a model of cheerful cynicism.

The cheer was genuine. He liked his job and his home life. He enjoyed his fellow human beings. He had a lively sense of humor.

The cynicism also was genuine. He knew all the angles and answers. He was confident that he discerned every motive, every attitude in others. Life was a long contest for comfort and advantage. That was about it.

At the time I felt a little sorry for him. I thought a part of him must be, despite his cheer, not really happy. With the perspective of years, I've decided I was off the mark. I think a part of him was simply vacant.

He had no capacity for reverence. By this I do not mean religious sensibility. I mean that he could view a great painting with interest but never with awe. He could look at the stars without a twinge of wonder. He was numb to the difference between fun and joy.

I thought I glimpsed his profile in an essay by the late anthropologist Loren Eiseley. He worried that twentieth-century Western culture was trivializing the human spirit. He feared the result could be imagined as a new category of Homo sapiens. He called it Asphalt Man.

I leave the term to imply what it will to others. I am not competent to elaborate on Dr. Eiseley's elegant thinking. In my own imagination, Asphalt Man takes several forms. Some of them annoy only me. Some amount to more—and worse.

I hear his voice in politicians who set out to meddle with great universities. This is happening in my state, among others. Politically connected policymakers have trimmed liberal arts programs deemed to be underused. During subsequent controversy, one policymaker was quoted as saying, "We are capitalists. We have to look at what the demand is, and we have to respond to the demand."

What to say of a statement that is at once so silly and so revealing? We should begin with first principles: education curricula are supposed to shape students, not vice-versa.

People now in control of our legislature want a turn toward job preparation in the university's mission. The talk of supply and demand is window dressing for a sharp change in policy. And it is a dodge past the truth that, had mere marketplace utility been their guide, great universities would not now be great.

My state has a history of systemic rural poverty. In levying and spending the taxes to build the university, leaders of yesteryear wanted to offer their constituents a path of escape from life behind a mule. And they wanted graduates equipped to do more than earn a buck. They knew that fine minds are as likely to be born into plowboys as anywhere else. They hoped graduates would build an economy, but they knew graduates would—for better or worse—build a society.

They would not have wanted their university to produce Asphalt Man. They would have recognized in him the heart of my former friend's cynicism: he valued only what he himself could understand. This was not merely an attitude. For him it was an ethic. Anything beyond his personal ken was not worth knowing.

He would have sniffed that programs of arts and letters were about frilly and superfluous notions. But in fact they are about the inner light that makes the human species unique.

Dr. Eiseley feared that Asphalt Man was capable of pawning treasures to improve the roads.

I fear that leaders in my state are offering to prove him right.

WHO DOES OUR KILLING?
JUNE 18, 2015

The Charleston massacre and the trial of the Colorado theater shooter have put me back in an old quandary While I am against the death penalty, I recognize that it is widely favored by people whose conscience is every bit as good as mine.

To my ear, their arguments begin roughly this way:

Claims that the death penalty lacks general deterrent impact are not persuasive. Yes, yes, studies say this and studies say that. But they depend on an inherently implausible notion. They purport to put a yardstick on nothingness—to measure how often unknown persons have made unknown, inner decisions against committing a crime, with the result that nothing happened.

And clearly, the death penalty deters the people upon whom it is visited. We can be sure that they will never repeat the crime of which they were convicted. Recidivism will not be a problem.

This view finds nourishment in a larger concern that our criminal justice system is a screen door against wind. While the concern can be overblown by hotheads and political opportunists, it is not without merit. The courts and the jails should reliably keep dangerous people off the street. They do not.

A crusty old friend of mine would here advance one more argument: society should not shrink from saying that some people are just bad actors and deserve what they get.

My friend had strong opinions and a vivid vocabulary. He liked to say we should be careful not to get so open-minded that our brains fall out. But on the matter of criminal penalties, he did have a point. Punishments have a societal value. We define our community in the rules we make. It is not merely appropriate for society to articulate ultimate prohibitions. It is important.

Stacked against the ultimate penalty of death are familiar assertions, all true: It is capriciously applied. It falls more heavily on minorities and the poor. Innocents may be convicted.

My own opposition is intractably simple. I try to imagine pushing the needle or flipping the switch with my own hand. I can't do it. If killing is wrong, we do not make it less wrong by hiring others to do it for us.

The trial of the Charleston shooter is yet to come. The trial of the Colorado monster already tests our patience and our nerve. There is no doubt of his guilt. And yet the process wears on at a huge cost of time and money.

Defense attorneys might counter that in defending the culprit, they are defending the system. Whatever penalty may be levied at the end of the process, it is important to reach the end by respecting our own rules. It is important that we not be a mob.

TAKING BACK OUR STATE
JUNE 25, 2015

News reports say former Governor Jim Hunt has convened a group to discuss "an alternative vision" for North Carolina. Let's hope they'll want to counteract the serial disgrace that began with the election of Gov. Pat McCrory and legislators widely beholden to a wealthy, right-wing ideologue.

Charlotte Mayor McCrory was a thoughtful, even-handed public servant. Governor McCrory has baffled his friends, appalled his critics, and saddened both. His political style has been long on parroting doctrinaire slogans. As the state's chief executive, he has displayed a startling capacity for connivance and double-talk.

Treated early in his tenure to vocal dismay, McCrory lashed out. He decried "scare tactics" from "the extreme left." Welcome to today's North Carolina. If you exercise a citizen's right to speak up, your own governor gives you the back of his hand.

Meanwhile, under iron control by Republicans, the legislature indulged the notion that might makes right. Lawmakers whooped through abortion restrictions and a high-tech poll tax. They have tainted the state's distinguished university with partisan politics.

The list of dismal particulars goes on. And while we might disagree on this specific or that one, they are alike in the spirit of their affront to principled governance: they are fundamentally out of tune with the long-manifest public temperament of this state.

North Carolina has comfortably hosted conservative political ideas and progressive ones, too. Our best leaders have honored a sleeves-up, pragmatic ethic of tending to essential knitting in the broad public interest.

The offense of our current leaders is regrettably simple. In imposing a stark, partisan lockstep on North Carolina, the governor and the legislature have functioned in contempt of their obligation to serve all the people.

Possibly, they have produced an especially significant result. They may have coalesced in the public mind the sort of resonating idea that supports a successful brand. In ironic justice, the brand would belong to their opponents.

Attorney General Roy Cooper embraced it as he put his own hat in the gubernatorial ring: "North Carolina is better than this."

AFTER THE FLAG
JULY 1, 2015

*The worst, the most corrupting lies are
problems wrongly stated.*

—Georges Bernanos

*Why, sometimes, I've believed as many as six impossible
things before breakfast.*

—The White Queen, in *Through The Looking Glass*

As a native Southerner, I say this about moves against the Confederate flag: Good riddance. It is a symbol of bigotry and, for some, a license to kill. It has no proper place in contemporary public life.

The general applause for these moves represents an ironic turn of events. Traditionally, on matters of race, the rest of the nation has liked to look away with scorn to Dixie. A sordid and shameful strain in this region's history has enabled selective recollection of history in other backyards: of segregated schools in the Northeast and upper Midwest, segregated public accommodations and even entire towns in New England, anti-miscegenation laws in most of the lower forty-eight states. And so on.

History will likely right itself in the long term. Meanwhile, we are left to deal with the realities of here and now. One of these is the ordinary human yen to think of racism as someone else's sin. Another is the temptation to believe that we may finally have the problem on the run—to feel good about melting the tip of an iceberg, in the case of the flag.

Still another can he heard among politicians and commentators on the right. They are signaling that they sense in their target constituency an issue-weariness on race. After the Charleston church massacre, they strained to avoid calling it what it was: a classic racial hate crime. In a bizarre aside, the editorialists at *The Wall Street Journal* thought it timely to assert that institutional racism no longer exists in America.

Without evidence that the White Queen works at *The Journal*, we may conclude that the editorialists don't get out much and that their office windows do not afford them a clear view of, say, the criminal justice system.

The politics and atmospherics of race have not been good these days. Politicians have worked openly to inhibit minority voting. Our African-American president has been mocked and reviled in some quarters, even by some in Congress. See, for example, the Norfolk, Nebraska, parade float portraying an outhouse as the Obama Presidential Library. See the collected sayings of John Boehner, Mitch McConnell, and Ted Cruz. (Senator Cruz's rhetoric is best sampled when there will be time afterward to take a shower.)

Notwithstanding White Queen commentators and pandering politicians, institutional racism is still alive. Minorities are disadvantaged in health care, even in access to grocery shopping. They have been afflicted by the banking, insurance, and mortgage industries. Racial disparity is sharply increasing in schools, especially in the urban Northeast.

To say that we are all responsible is not to say that we are all bigots. It is, rather, to say that we are not always attentive to what is produced or permitted by the accretion of our everyday behaviors.

Symbols matter. Rejecting a hateful symbol matters. But symbolism can't substitute for the glamourless work of diligent citizenship: for listening when we're told that minority schools are flagging a few miles from our homes, for remembering that the politicians passing those ugly voting laws were elected from polling places like the one down the street.

COMIC POLITICS
JULY 8, 2015

No Republican presidential candidate has yet been pictured in a propeller beanie, but Donald Trump probably has trouble with hats of any sort. In kindness we might call the Republican field colorful. In candor we would call most of it dreadful.

Parts of it may fall out this way:

Some hothouse flowers of state politics will not do well in the great outdoors. One of these will be former Texas Gov. Rick Perry, who still doesn't seem to get it: much of the country doesn't care how they do things down yonder in the Lone Star State. His indictment will matter less than his tin ear.

Another will be Wisconsin's bully-boy governor, Scott Walker. Even when he's not bumbling, he will struggle to he heard over cries of outrage and dismay from his own state.

Still another will be Gov. Chris Christie of New Jersey, who may need more than one closet to hold all his skeletons. He struts his in-your-face act with such gusto that one writer calls him Gov.

Powder Keg. He will discover that blunt talk is like virginity. People admire it more in the abstract. Close and constant national scrutiny will show him to be a poseur—or, as his home folks are beginning to say, a phony.

Elsewhere in the pack are long shots getting makeovers for the national audience; scolds offering a dog's breakfast of pet peeves; and wannabes who may only wanna follow the Sarah Palin pattern of celebrity, in which flamboyantly failed candidates can make a good living as political hams.

Experts see front-runners in Florida's Sen. Marco Rubio and former Florida governor Jeb Bush. Rubio gained his Senate seat by surviving a multicandidate election in which more people voted against him than for him. He has traveled well on youth and ethnicity, but on matters of substance, he has sometimes been a dim star. Does he have genuine political ability? So far we don't really know.

Some early support migrated to Bush simply for want of attractive options. And he has not yet found a stride. Meanwhile, examinations of his past show him standing close to some shady business deals and making a living by trading on his family name. In other words, there are shadows on his character and his competence.

Nowhere in sight is a rescuer who will say the truth about the national GOP: The emperor is naked. The party's best talents are mediocre. Their pretense to stewardship of conservatism is a shame and a reminder that an idea is not responsible for everyone who claims it. In the history of Western democracy, the role of authentic conservative thought has been honorable and useful. In today's American politics, the role of the Republican Party has sometimes been neither.

The GOP needs to free itself of people who treat politics as playacting and the party as a means of hustling a buck or grinding an ax.

HANGOVER AHEAD?
JULY 17, 2015

He had, in fact, got everything from the church and Sunday School, except, perhaps, any longing whatever for decency and kindness and reason.

—Sinclair Lewis, *Elmer Gantry*

Congress shall make no law respecting an establishment of religion…

—*From the First Amendment to the United States Constitution*

People who behave foolishly are apt to be deemed fools. People who wield power foolishly are apt to be deemed dangerous fools.

—*Anonymous*

Mixing politics and religion adulterates both and produces an unhealthy brew. More's the pity that foes of same-sex marriage are tippling on it.

Republican politicians woo the religious right with talk of writing God into the Constitution. Megapreachers rail against the Supreme Court, the president, even against citizens who voted for the president. State and local officials offer religious excuses for obstruction and foot-dragging. That old-time religion has never had so many fans.

I'm not among them. To my ear, the voice of the far Christian right has always been a little long on judging and a little short on loving. And in any case, it is a factional voice. It does not typify Christian thought, much less American public attitude. Yet some on that side would see their favorite doctrines written into civil law, to be enforced on all comers.

History warns against thinking to evangelize by the sword. And common sense warns against thinking to dance with the devil and come away clean. Except perhaps to unusually obtuse children, the principle of the thing is simple. If government were empowered to favor one version of faith over others, no one's faith would be safe.

Yet between the preachers and the pols, a fond dalliance proceeds. On both sides, temptation has worked its powerful way.

Without a coherent vision of public policy for the country, the Republican Party is doubly open to single-issue, hot-button politics. On the religious right, a worldly appetite for political power is at work. When candidates go a-courtin' over there, they can find the welcome warm indeed. And over there can be found a politician's dream of cohesive voter blocs ripe for sloganeering. Thus we see religion used to decorate the hoary tactic of barren politicians: demonize a minority.

The same-sex marriage issue will burn out eventually. It is at odds with settled law and public opinion. But the mutual exploitation of preachers and pols may linger for a while. The appetite for it on the religious right is plain to see. And the GOP's problem remains. The party has little to say to the American people—and leaders who say even that much badly. Thus Republican candidates will be tempted toward the expedient of whooping up emotional issues.

They won't succeed in turning the country into a theocracy. They will succeed in debasing the language of our politics.

FAITH IN THE CLOSET
AUGUST 5, 2015

U sually I dislike sermons. The form is lost on me. This has occasioned some awkwardness in my life, as I've had good friends among clergy. They in turn have compounded my problem by being exceptions who vividly proved the rule. It is a mildly uncomfortable conundrum.

In any case, I usually dislike sermons. But I perked up at one a few Sundays ago. The preacher began with a story of visiting a backyard barbecue at a neighbor's house. One of the other guests, on learning that he was a clergyman, treated him to a lecture. It began with words on the order of, "Do you really believe all that stuff?" It ended with words on the order of, "You can't prove any of it."

The story resonated with me. From time to time, I have a layman's version of the same experience. People who are not religious seem to be bothered by the fact that I am.

I take care not to wear religion on my sleeve. But I don't dissemble. If the subject comes up in social conversation, and the question lands in my lap, I acknowledge being observant in a Christian denomination. Several kinds of reaction may occur. Some people shoot embarrassed glances toward far corners of the room, as if I had claimed to be a chicken pot pie. Others go blank and silent, as if to forbear through rudeness. Still others go rigid with something that looks very like annoyance.

Granted, religion can nowadays be a cringeworthy subject. Choose your culprit, starting with the scalawags who will cure your bunions or save your soul—your choice—if only you'll pony up. At the other extreme are the sweet folks whose faith is utterly sincere and comprehensively vocal. Nobody likes to be harangued. I'd rather not be blessed by the cashier at the grocery store.

In between, we have hatemongers, politicians who claim God as an ally, and megapreachers whose definition of reverent humility permits them million-dollar homes. Praise the Lord, pass the loot, vote for me, and scorn the neighbor of your choice.

To all the above, I plead not guilty. Even so, I may wind up being—figuratively speaking—the guy who stops conversation by telling the wrong joke or grinning with spinach between his teeth.

Perhaps it is not irrelevant that atheism has become stylish. It has its own megapreachers and proselytizers. And like my friends on the religious side, its adherents can be artfully selective about which tenets they embrace and which they ignore. I particularly enjoy the Christmas season's manger scene mania, in which religious tradition must not put so much as a toe on secular turf. I wait for the manger police to reject the tradition of taking the Christian Sabbath as a day off from work. So far, no go.

With the rest of the human race, I am capable of petty resentment. I do become annoyed in those moments when I realize I'm being regarded as a walking, talking faux pas. In years past I might venture to talk my way through them. The result was always social disaster. I babbled earnest endorsements of the theory of evolution and abject admissions of scriptural contradiction until I sounded as if I were selling door-to-door magazine subscriptions. I embarrassed whole rooms full of people, including myself.

Social mores are bearable, if not always sensible. But the ones here at hand reflect a larger context that I think terribly sad. The hucksters and pols and zealots have so thoroughly poisoned the vocabulary of religion that it is genuinely risky to mention the subject in polite company.

As for my social life, perhaps I will try to hint—without actually fibbing—that I am a Druid.

And come to think of it, I wonder if Druids have sermons.

MIRROR, MIRROR ON THE WALL
AUGUST 13, 2015

An old friend used to call them The Baddies. They are the kinds of days when things go wrong from the start. You oversleep. Breakfast is rushed. Some of it gets stuck between your teeth. Then you get toothpaste on your sleeve. That kind of day. Bad karma right out of the gate.

I've thought of The Baddies as the presidential campaigns lurch to a start. Of Republicans, we can at most say that their dueling publicity stunts have offered counterpoint to the yawnfest on the Democratic side. Over there, while Hillary Clinton still seems the one to beat, tepid poll numbers say that even supporters are not enthusiastic about her.

At this rate, our next president will be sent to the White House by people voting with their fingers crossed. Such are the possibilities of politics in a safe, affluent country. We have evolved but not improved our definition of the phrase "consent of the governed." The first Continental Congress received its consent in an affirmative sense of the word. It had no established authority within the norms of the day. It was sent to do the work of the people who did the sending. Nowadays, government has vested interests of its own. It is large beyond any valid need. It is extravagantly wasteful of the public's money. And it is peopled by careerists who are serenely confident of the rightness of their judgments for the rest of us.

This should be fertile ground for Republican politicians, who do indeed like to prattle about limited government. However, it is only prattle. In saying they'd like to scale back government enterprise, they mean they'd like to scale back government enterprise to someone else's constituents. When it comes to sending boodle to the home folks, Republicans are champs. The day of truly limited government is over in this country, and this is why politicians who preach it sound so often callous or silly.

According to the news-celebrities who call their opinions analysis, time favors Democrats, because their natural constituencies are growing. But which Democrats does time favor? Consider what the Bernie Sanders phenomenon reveals: a candidate who has remarkably energized voters is a renegade by established political norms.

These norms have given the Democrats Hillary Clinton. In her, a talent for policy is evident. A personal gift for politics is not. Direct conversations with the people are visibly a chore. Thus her campaign seeks to reduce political leadership to an exercise in packaging and posturing. (Note to Clinton staff: lose the official photo that makes her look as if she's been startled out of a nap.)

And so, on both sides of the partisan divide, we find today's chosen vehicle for obtaining the consent of the governed: politics by marketable pose. This is what we get when we mix show business into public affairs. (See: Donald Trump.) Also, this is what we get from candidates who don't quite know what to say to the American people. We are beset by would-be leaders who are quite willing to tell us what they think we want to hear, if only they can figure out what that is.

Along with ineptitude—or because of it—not a few of the candidates have a second deficiency. They have embraced the notion of political doctrine as higher truth. Some of them appear actually to believe this. For others, claiming to have the one true vision is a shortcut past the labor of crafting a coherent program of governance from the competing values of a diverse society.

A lack of political aptitude is a serious shortcoming in candidates for an office that is, foremost, a position of political leadership. Some of this country's highest achievements in democracy have gone forward on the sweaty shoulders of political craft. The nation can negotiate many circumstances with a mere manager in the White House, but moments inescapably come when it needs a leader.

DUCKING THE BIG QUESTION
AUGUST 27, 2015

First the story; then the point:

The young man was full of himself, in the way young men can be. He was puffed up with his new scientific graduate degree. And his girlfriend was listening. He was showing off.

He announced to fellow dinner guests (who had not raised the subject) that the Christian gospels are so much hooey. Full of discrepancies and contradictions. Not even close to the standards of real history. Written one hundred years after the events they purport to record, by persons unknown who could not have been eyewitnesses.

Our young lecturer did not know that the earliest Christian scriptures were written eighteen to twenty years after the events of Jesus's life. They are Pauline letters. More to the point, these letters were written by Paul to congregations already up and running across the region. In the bosom of an ancient theocracy, something fundamental had happened. It had caused people in numbers to abandon their very concept of reality, even at the risk of their lives.

Our young dinner lecturer, being thus uninformed, had no occasion to consider some points of simple fact: The existence of the man Paul is settled. The authenticity of the main body of his letters is settled. In these letters he says he did business with the apostle Peter and Jesus's brother James. He says he met people who had encountered the resurrected Jesus. And he says he met the resurrected Jesus himself.

Had our lecturer known as much, he would have faced a decision: where would he place the information on a yardstick of credibility? At one extreme, he would conclude that the man Paul gave his life to propagate a cockamamie yarn among folks indulging a mass delusion. At the opposite pole, he would conclude that Paul knew what he was talking about and meant what he said.

That's the story. Here's the point:

The young lecturer has brethren in attitude. Our rational and enlightened age hosts a mode of thinking that is neither. It embraces an ethic of skepticism that questions everything but itself. It swallows whole the doctrine that faith and reason are foes. It tolerates and even celebrates a certain kind of cultural ignorance.

Holding the Christian gospels to standards of modern history is simply silly. The discipline of modern history did not exist at the time of the gospel writings. Judged knowledgeably and objectively, the case for the historicity of the Christian gospels is sound. The evidence is available to anyone who knows how to read and bothers to look.

But we moderns don't do a lot of bothering. Our reasons may seem good-hearted.

We are put off by the loons and scoundrels who caricature religion to their own benefit. Or we are put off by rulemongers who use the Bible to push what one writer calls "a narrow, hard and exclusive piety." Or we are confident of pursuing morality without religion.

Or we're just too modern and too skeptical. In the upshot, a wise and beautiful book languishes at the outskirts of cultural literacy, and supposedly discerning people tap-dance past the essential question about Judeo-Christian scripture. The question is not whether the Bible describes an elevated system of morality. The question is whether it tells a story that is, in its essence, true.

Ultimate questions can be mercilessly simple, and so can the decisions they imply.

True? Or false?

Yes? Or no?

On this question, our rational age has not dealt rationally with the fact that automatic skepticism amounts to a lazy form of evasion. Our young lecturer hadn't dealt rationally with it, either. For intellectual rigor, poor marks all around.

A WINTER LAMENT
SEPTEMBER 20, 2015

Snowflakes are kisses from heaven.

—Anonymous

Winter is nature's way of saying, "Up yours."

—Robert Byrne

Serious people, in my view, should pause now and then to consider the great divides in the human family. Not mere race or religion or nationality. We should consider the fundamentals that sort us out, to wit:

- Some people are cheerful in the morning; some are not.
- Some people are always on time; some are always late.
- Some people are tidy. Some others don't bother.
- Some people embrace winter; some hate it.

The first three of these fundamentals do share one characteristic: people on opposite sides of them marry each other with regularity. This produces tensions and struggles of which much has been written and nothing more need be ventured here. Thus we are left to consider the matter of wintertime.

Winter people are a cheerful and energetic bunch. They see jewels in snowflakes. They love the textures of winter clothing and the hearty warmth of a good winter soup. They even go outdoors, to skate and ski and sled. Do they shiver, do they fall, do they suffer the least discomfort? Never.

Anti-winter people, on the other hand, are morose and disagreeable for several months a year. I can say this with assurance, as I am one of them. For us, winter is chilblains, wet socks, and cold drafts that follow us through the house no matter where we sit. Presented with hearty soup and a hot toddy, we long for summer tomatoes and a gin and tonic. In winter's endless darkness, we brood about deeper questions, such as: can there really be any excuse for the month of February?

I have these matters in mind because the forecasters are beginning to remind us that winter is around the corner. And they say it will be a bad one. Here I do not rely on the folks employed by the government weather service, although they should be credited at least with enterprise. Apparently they've discovered how to generate computer models by rolling dice.

No, I listen to forecasts that are tried and true—such as the ones from the *Old Farmers' Almanac*. This year's winter outlook is a stinker. Lots of cold. Lots of snow, even in places that don't usually get it. Lots of rain in places that won't get snow. In other words, chills and slipping and sliding and slop. Just about everywhere.

Of course, even good forecasters are not perfect, and so I permit myself hope for a bit of reprieve from this vision of doom. I wait on tiptoe for the next major prediction—the October pronouncement of the woolly worms. These caterpillars are colored with bands of brown and black. If brown predominates when they emerge in the fall, the winter will be mild. If black predominates, hunker down for a bad one.

And what if the almanac and the worms do indeed give opposite predictions? I'll go with the optimistic one, of course, even knowing that its reprieve is only partial. I will be spared a measure of dread as the season approaches. But I won't be spared some features of even the mildest winters. Drab skies giving way to long hours of darkness. Bare, skeletal trees. And the big one: the clueless cheer of people who won't stop chattering that they enjoy the season.

I insist that I am not unreasonable in this outlook. It's the way some of us are made. In fact we are recognized in literature. When Ishmael, in *Moby-Dick*, wanted an image for comprehensive gloom, he said he had November in his soul.

Indeed.

So there.

DOES THIS POPE REALLY MATTER?
OCTOBER 11, 2015

My friend is gratified but not overwhelmed by Pope Francis's groundbreaking style. He says he'll believe real change is afoot when the Catholic Church gives all its treasure to the poor and sets up headquarters in a pole barn.

My friend is not given to jaundiced views. But neither is he given to glossing over fundamentals. Pope Francis has abandoned none of the harder doctrines that have troubled his denomination and divided public attitude. In its blood and bones, the Catholic Church remains itself.

Yet this pope has caused a surge of reaction among Catholics, Protestants, and even people who might deem themselves irreligious. Pundits parse his words. Analysts try to peer inside his head and heart.

What is going on here?

One commentator says Pope Francis has changed the tune, if not the words. And the new tune has resonated with people of all sorts. Or startled them. In an age that politicizes nearly every human transaction (and thus adulterates any useful understanding of politics), the Pope is commonly rated on a liberal/conservative scale. But I think a better measure of his impact may lie elsewhere. My hunch is that he has galvanized attention because his demeanor of loving, inclusive humility clashes with widely shared perceptions of the established church—Protestant and Catholic alike.

Consider the not-incidental context. Church affiliation is in broad decline. People have been voting with their feet. Dorothy L. Sayers, who wrote far more than crime fiction, ventured an explanation. In a collection of essays called *Letters to a Diminished Church,* she suggests that the church is complicit in the accretion of a damaging image of Christian faith.

She offers a mock catechism. An abbreviated sample:

What does the church think of God the father? He is omnipotent and holy. He created the world and imposed on man conditions impossible of fulfillment; he is very angry if these are not carried out...

What was Jesus Christ like in real life? He was a good man— so good as to be called the Son of God...He had no sense of humor...If we try to live like him, God the Father will let us off being damned hereafter and only have us tortured in this life.

What is meant by atonement? God wanted to damn everybody, but his vindictive sadism was sated by the crucifixion of his own Son, who was quite innocent and therefore a particularly attractive victim...

What does the church think of sex? God made it necessary to the machinery of the world and tolerates it provided the parties are (a) married and (b) get no pleasure out of it.

What does the church call sin? Sex (otherwise than as ex-cepted above); getting drunk; saying "damn"; murder; and cruelty to dumb animals; not going to church; most kinds of amusement. "Original sin" means that anything we enjoy doing is wrong.

What is faith? Resolutely shutting your eyes to scientific fact.

What are the seven Christian virtues? Respectability, child-ishness, mental timidity, dullness, sentimentality, censori-ousness and depression of spirits.

Sayers continues:

Somehow or other, and with the best of intentions, we have shown the world the typical Christian in the likeness of a crashing and rather ill-natured bore...

Let us in heaven's name drag out the divine drama from under the dreadful accumulation of slipshod thinking and trashy sentiment heaped upon it...

We should be careful here. Organized religion is vulnerable to caricature. Friends favor images that are easy to swallow. Foes favor images that are easy to condemn. The truth lies elsewhere and is as complex as life.

The record of the church through the ages is therefore mixed. And while the mix plentifully includes sacrificial service of good by exemplars of the highest kind, I think today's church does de-serve charges of complicity in its own struggles. Pope Francis's denomination remains itself. Its doctrines on birth control and abortion, to name only two, are a direct cause of much suffering. Other denominations favor their various versions of narrow, judg-mental, and exclusionary piety.

Today's church at large displays a taste for rulemongering and doctrinal calisthenics. In this it is an edifice made with hands, and it reflects human foibles all too clearly. Add to this in some quarters an unseemly appetite for political power, and we come to a melancholy juncture: people of clear mind and good heart can feel that the posture of the established church is out of tune with the spirit of the Christian gospels.

This formulation necessarily presupposes an appetite—or at least a respect—for the spirit of the Christian gospels. We cannot be offended by abuse of an ethic we hold in no regard.

And so along comes Pope Francis, who reveals something in us by touching it. Millions are energized by his example of loving, inclusive humility.

I think the phenomenon is not trivial.

BAD LANGUAGE
NOVEMBER 2, 2015

I paused when my *New York Times* advised me of it. A prominent businessman had fatally brained himself falling off a treadmill. The incident, my *Times* informed me from its very front page, had sent a shiver of concern through "the fitness community."

Now, the regulars at my own gym might charitably be called a diverse bunch. We have middle-aged wheezers who aren't as fit as they imagine they used to be. We have deskbound office workers laboring to contain their waistlines. We have oldsters trying to preserve enough flexibility to reach into the far depths of the liquor cabinet. And we have a sprinkling of impossibly buff youngsters who dart and glide among the rest of us as if we were statues.

I daresay that we are reasonably typical gym folk. And I would never have foreseen these motley groups being called a community. Beneath my notice, the steady creep of English usage had established a new frontier. This was the real nugget of news in the *Times* article. For those of us who hadn't been paying attention, with it were implied new defining questions.

Question 1: In this new vocabulary, what constitutes a community? Can it be any area of shared interest? Several of my friends especially enjoy hummus. Are they a hummus community? Would voyeurs now be called the peeping community? Gossips the dishing community?

Or perhaps the test is one of size. Must a group reach a certain critical mass to be eligible for community status?

An excursion through the world of collective nouns was not helpful on the point. Mathematicians, apparently with time on their hands, have coined a host of words for numbers of special size. One whopper, for example, is called a googolplexplexplexminex. As the numbers themselves are impossible to comprehend, the utility of these terms escapes me.

Traditional usage offers a variety of terms for groups of animals. Notable among them, through some sources, is "a congress of baboons." Other sources dispute this as bogus lexicography. Still others reject it as a slander upon baboons. Absent authoritative ruling, we seem to be free to arrive at our own opinions.

Groups of human beings seemed a likelier focus. There we find troupes, teams, squads, slates, arrays, and congregations. One source quite seriously lists a melody of harpists, a pint of Irishmen, and an explosion of Italians.

My research failed, however, to find parameters for the latest concepts of community. Apparently any group larger than two may be so called. This does present possibilities of a sort. People who text while driving might be deemed the fathead community. Telemarketers would be members of the pest community.

But this kind of freewheeling usage robs language of essential meaning and moves it into the hands of...well, the jargon community. And come to think of it, I guess people given to this particular form of jargon could be called the community community.

Enough said. It's making me a member of the grumpy community. Perhaps I'll find allies at the gym, if I can interest some folks who are not too winded to discuss it.

HO, HO...HO?
DECEMBER 5, 2015

We've had a little dust-up in our town. One of our big shopping malls decided to update the setting where Santa makes his appearances. They replaced the Christmas tree with a high-tech, interactive replica of a glacier. Howls went up, and mall management soon promised to return the tree.

'Tis the season when peace and goodwill can be episodically scant. Absent a major new wrinkle in the fabric of space-time, we'll soon see disputes over manger scenes and more wrangles over the use and even the nomenclature of symbolic holiday trees. Some folks will complain that the proper spirit of the holidays has been compromised by materialism. Others will push back against religious overtones.

My friend Harry watches with wry amusement. He likes to consider himself an armchair philosopher. Harry says some of the stuff that goes on during the holidays is like a family squabble.

Being human, Harry does have Christmas grumbles of his own. Being a philosopher, Harry favors grumbles that are thoughtful. One of them features the "Panhandlers." These are the people with bells and buckets who post themselves at public entrances and, with relentlessly cheerful demeanor, challenge passersby to proceed without giving. Harry is especially irked by those whose station outside liquor stores implies doctrinal disapproval of demon rum.

He responds with an animated refusal to give. He embraces his supply of demon rum and answers the bell-ringer's hearty greeting with an aggressively hearty one of his own. Harry says that neither one of them really means it. Deep down, the bell-ringer thinks Harry is a heathen skinflint. Not so deep down, Harry hopes the bell-ringer's feet are cold.

Harry is not, in fact, a heathen skinflint. He is a churchman. He has his own spiritual concept of the season and doesn't want bell-ringers pushing theirs upon him. In this, he says, he can see the desire of irreligious friends to celebrate the season in their own way. But being a philosopher, Harry adds a caveat: the proselytizing impulse points in all directions; those friends who like to skip religious notions would be happier if he did, too.

And so goes the season. Holiday stresses, they test us, every one. We expect that public venues will be flooded with treacly music and that one neighbor couple will festoon their house with garish lights. We know that Uncle Wilbur will have too much eggnog and drone the same old stories. Aunt Pearl's Jell-O salad will be dreadful. Cousin Fawn's children will be impossible. The in-laws will keep score on our time with them. And what, oh what, to give cranky old Grandma?

Still, as Harry might say, you can't have a family squabble unless you have a family. Perhaps our Christmas grumbles are like Uncle Wilbur's stories: tiresome but also comfortably familiar. Yes, I wish one house in our neighborhood did not resemble an interstate truck stop at night, but I drive by to see it anyway. Yes, I wish that Frosty and Rudolph would run far away together. But not until my grandchildren have grown up.

The unifying thread in all the holiday kerfuffle is this: most of us, in our own chosen way, care. I'll take the season in all its various parts.

And I'll give Grandma a gift card. She'll like the control.

SHAMING, BLAMING, AND LOVE
DECEMBER 22, 2015

It is, no doubt, impossible to prevent his praying for his
mother, but we have ways of rendering the prayers innocuous.
Make sure that they are always very "spiritual," that he is
always concerned with the state of her soul and never with her
rheumatism.

—The demon Screwtape, counseling the apprentice
demon Wormwood in C. S. Lewis's *The Screwtape Letters.*

My friend Harry wonders why God does not stop wars and disease and natural disasters. He is slower to wonder why God doesn't stop him from being envious or unkind. Like most of us, Harry is selectively interested in God's to-do list. Also, he's been habituated by our convenience culture. When he does consider a divine agenda, he may rest with thinking that it should just be more like his own.

Harry is aware of these ironies. In a mellow mood, he cites himself as evidence that the Almighty has a tolerant sense of humor. Harry is a bit of an armchair philosopher. He savors irony, and he enjoys rubbing ideas together.

In fact, truth to tell, he enjoys a bit of an argument now and then. Certain kinds of opportunities make his antennae go right up. High among them are social conversations where someone introduces the subject of religion for purposes of debunking it. Harry loves to expound on these episodes. He does it roughly this way:

You can see them getting ready to bring it (Harry says), almost like a dare. They say just enough to get the subject on the table, and then they declare something along the lines of, "Well, I just don't believe it." It's like they think God is over in the corner with his hand up, waiting to be recognized.

I take the bait every time (Harry says). Just can't help it. I mean, religion is someone's private business, but claptrap is claptrap. They will say they are nonbelievers, and I will say, well, since it's obviously impossible to believe nothing at all, what you really are is a disbeliever. So, I say, tell me what it is that you don't believe.

And they will dribble out a bunch of stuff that sounds like they scavenged leftovers from some of those hairstyled televangelists. And we will back and forth a bit until we get that nonsense sort of pushed out of the way, and we get down to where they have to do more than snipe at other people's views, and they have to take ownership of something on their own. Then, they will say something like, "I believe there is no God."

And I say, well, that is certainly your personal business, but I think it's very interesting that, even so, you are willing to make a declaration of faith, which is what you just did.

It chaps their cheeks every time, and I love it (Harry says). Just can't help it.

Harry has a mischievous streak. But in what he has to say, there is a worthwhile nugget. A certain amount of what's nowadays peddled as divine message is, in fact, human contrivance. It is wildly out of tune with the manifest spirit of Judeo-Christian scripture.

In it we can search in vain for the emphasis on social justice that begins with the Old Testament prophets. In it we can search in vain for the kind of thoughtful love reflected in a statement of welcome published by a parish church in my state. It says, in part:

- We understand and believe that faith is a matter of mind as well as heart, and that taking the Bible seriously means it need not always be taken literally.
- We believe God's love embraces all persons equally, no matter their gender, race, or sexual orientation...We believe diversity, acceptance, and inclusivity are strengths to be taught.
- We believe it is important to find ways to treat all people with integrity and respect.
- We believe...that the social expression of love is justice.

Harry can be quite colorful on the subject, especially if he's had a couple of drinks:

I've been a churchgoer for fifty years (Harry says). I've seen people shucking and jiving past the hard parts and talking a lot better game than they played. Hell, I've seen a fair handful of preachers talking a better game than they played. But you know what it is, mostly? It's ordinary folks doing the best they can and working hard to figure out what that's supposed to be.

The right parts of it are nothing near the kind of loudmouthed shaming and blaming that you hear so much of nowadays. That stuff is just plain wrong. And you know what's the telltale thing? Politicians have latched onto it. Politicians who are all about taking sides. Us against them. And free lunch, too. Easy answers.

You just sign onto these rules that I stand for, and never mind where they came from; you stand with me against those people over there, and everything will work out just fine.

You want to strain your brain? (Harry says.) Try to imagine a politician running on a platform of loving your neighbor. That loving your neighbor business is tough work. At least it is for me. You have to be willing to give a little of yourself away. It's a lot easier to call on God to fix the state of things than to think about how you might belly up to helping with it yourself. So, imagine a politician running on that kind of message:

Elect me, and I will call upon you to love your neighbor, even the one who's a nasty son of a gun. I will call upon you to give a little of yourself away. You. Yes, you.

Fat chance (Harry says).

Harry would cringe if accused of theology. He would insist that a lifetime of churchgoing has come up far short of making him any kind of saint. He would declare himself grateful for that divine sense of humor. He would say he's an ordinary guy doing the best he can and working hard to figure out what that's supposed to be.

I would say that some of Harry's figuring is pretty good.

IN PRAISE OF STORIES
JANUARY 21, 2016

I n what follows, the names have been changed to protect the innocent, one of them being me. Everything else is true. These old newspaper stories are fun, I think. And at the end they may make a worthwhile point. In any case, here they are.

I remember: Joe, who would sometimes report for work in the newsroom wearing chinos, a T-shirt, and a floor-length black opera cape. (Crimson lining. He made bold fashion statements, our Joe.) He was a hell-raiser and an oddball and a damn good sportswriter. He could make you feel like you'd been at the game yourself.

I remember: Jimmy, who could make a story sing, oh my. But sometimes the words just wouldn't come, and Jimmy had a volcanic temper. Once, when his typewriter was especially balky, he opened a third-floor window and threw it into the parking lot below.

I remember: Clarence, an affably cranky old fellow. He was a hasty, two-finger typist who chewed paper when he wrote. Sometimes his fingers and his mind operated on different pages. Editors learned to watch his copy closely for such locutions as "sharper than the hangman's ax" and "now, the worm is on the other foot."

I remember: Eddie, who one year was conspicuously late returning to his desk from the company's Christmas buffet. He cheerfully confessed that he had taken extra time to boff a business-office clerk on an empty boardroom table. Jimmy liked to write at length. Advised that a piece was too long, he would simply narrow the margins on his typewriter and turn the same thing back in. It never worked, but Jimmy never stopped trying.

I remember: Bob, who once lost his grip in an argument with a newsroom colleague. He coated the colleague's desktop with rubber cement and set it on fire. The desk was metal, and the fire quickly burned out. But the smell was a problem for a while.

I remember: Betty, who cheerfully believed that her little bungalow was haunted. She toppled barriers of gender and industry caste by the sheer power of her inborn talent. She wrote her way out of a proofreader's job, into newsroom work, and on to publication as a novelist. Through it all she remained that rarest of creatures, a genuinely loving and generous human being. I thought that maybe Betty wrote like an angel because she was one.

Among such folks as these, I began my newspaper career. They all had their own quirks and styles, but they had one thing in common: the stuff they put in the newspaper had warm blood in its veins. From them I learned to understand the admonition: "A good newspaper doesn't print articles. It prints stories."

I'm not sure when the notion got afoot that our craft would be improved if it were "professionalized." But the notion did get afoot—and get away with us. Hiring fads favored sober-sided kids with academic pedigrees and superior attitudes. Hither and yon, newspapers were handed over to executives who were not really newspaper editors but process managers for information and entertainment marketing. Newspapers printed articles and talked *at* their communities rather than *with* them.

I suppose these observations sound like the maundering of a codger who misses the good old days. Well, they are, I am, and I do. But maybe they also say something useful about the factors that made newspapers moribund. Were powerful competitive and economic forces mounting against us? Yes. Was decline inevitable? Probably. But I think we were culpable, too. I think we greased the skids by turning our newspapers into mere merchandise and imagining ourselves a class above and apart. We became prissy neighbors in love with the sound of our own voices.

That's my own take. Colleagues from yesteryear might prefer the earthier verdict of a distinguished national reporter, the late Richard Ben Cramer. In the late nineties he surveyed the landscape of American journalism and lamented that it had been "overtaken by a Biblical plague of dickheads."

Anyhow, we did a pretty good job in our day. And I came away with a trove of stories.

Buy me a drink, and I'll tell you a few:

- About the young man who careened through the wee hours, searching in vain for a cop to help him with the naked, love-crazed young woman clinging to the hood of his car. (In the end they were briefly jailed by baffled authorities who couldn't figure out what else to do.)
- About the US senator who offered—on Senate letterhead—to punch me in the mouth. (He never succeeded, but he offered more than once.)
- About the time in our city-hall bureau when Frank lost patience with mouthy Al. Frank tied him to an overhead pipe by his necktie and left him standing tiptoe on a desktop. (Al was soon found and freed by the city manager, who left clucking and shaking his head. He never asked a thing about it.)

Oh, my word, the stories.

Heck, you don't even have to buy me a drink.

ON DRIFTING APART
FEBRUARY 17, 2016

A letter to the mavens of American marketing:

Dear Mavens,

I tell you this with a heavy heart. In fact, I have avoided saying it for quite a while. But a time comes when we should be honest. And so I must tell you that…

You may be losing me.

There is no animus in this. No collection of festering grievances. I am not angry, only confused. I no longer understand how you want me to respond.

It began with the cars. I am baffled by the naming of the models. When they were called Impalas and Firebirds, I got it. I caught the spirit of your temptation.

But now?

I found myself in traffic the other day with an Elantra. It crossed my mind to wonder: What am I to make of a car that could have been named for the heroine of a comic opera? (Furthermore, while I was woolgathering over that, I missed the light.)

And what about those alphanumeric designations? They are everywhere. In the established lexicon of letters and numbers, the letter X seems to be big. My own car is an XC60. I have no idea what this means. Am I supposed to feel that I have a better model than one called, say, AB29? Or should I yearn to own an XX1000? I don't know, because I have never asked. I have never asked, because I don't care. For your purposes, alas, I am simply numb to the appeal of the letter X.

In other examples, naming mysteries have reached into the restaurant trade. After all, what should I expect of the fare at a place called the Rusty Onion? At the Purple Pea, I'm probably not interested no matter what the offering.

And so on. You get the idea. I have episodes of being unsure what I'm supposed to want.

And do you know what makes them worse? The flashbacks. Browsing through a catalog not long ago, I was arrested—stopped cold—by the Fat Max Extreme AntiVibe Rip Claw Nailing Hammer.

The telltale thing here is, I don't really need a hammer. I have a perfectly serviceable hammer. I have never known it to vibrate.

Not so far.

But you see, the people who named the Fat Max knew how to get to the Guy Thing. One of the enduring tenets of Guy Nation is: You have to have the right tools for a job. And if you don't—well, who knows? The ad for the Fat Max awakened in me an urge to get right with Guy Nation. To repair something. Perhaps even to build.

Now, I can hear you saying, "Oh yes, but this fellow is some kind of rube. He is not a marketing expert." This is true. I am not a marketing expert. I am, however, one of your customers. And let's face it: the economy depends on your stimulating us to buy goods and services that we don't really need. Yet here am I, suffering bouts of Stimulus Interruptus.

It's sad for our relationship, but it's true. I had to tell you.

A time comes when we should be honest.

WAKEUP CALL?
MARCH 13, 2016

Congress shall make no law respecting an establishment of religion, or prohibiting the free exercise thereof; or abridging the freedom of speech, or of the press; or the right of the people peaceably to assemble, and to petition the government for a redress of grievances.

—First Amendment to the Constitution of the United States

My brand became more famous as I became more famous, and more opportunities presented themselves.

—Donald Trump

It doesn't matter what I do. People need to hear what I have to say. There's no one else who can say what I can say. It doesn't matter what I live.

—*Newt Gingrich*

Money is the mother's milk of politics.

—*Jesse "Big Daddy" Unruh*

I don't care what the newspapers say about me as long as they spell my name right.

—*Attributed to P. T. Barnum and various others*

The price of apathy towards public affairs is to be ruled by evil men.

—*Plato*

Viewed whole, the Constitution's guarantee of press freedom is a citizens' right, not an institutional right.

The founders could scarcely have foreseen the newspaper empires of the nineteenth and twentieth centuries. Less could they have known that television news would introduce the values of show business. And who would have guessed that, in the equivalent of a wink, the Internet would transform communication and turn the news of the day into a gumbo of fact, propaganda, vaudeville, and gossip?

In the new information age (here we'll tolerate today's loose use of the term "information"), retail commerce and politics have undergone a similar change. In both realms, vendors can bypass traditional brokers and reach the consuming public directly.

Being unable to lick 'em, traditional brokers have had to join 'em. On political fronts, mainstream news outlets cover a blizzard of tweets, blog blasts, Facebook rants, and cable news flaps. Major newspapers carry regular features auditing their own content and advising readers that some of what they've already reported is, upon examination, simply not true. Nowadays, not only Alice's Wonderland Queen may have occasion to believe six unbelievable things before breakfast.

If money has long been the mother's milk of politics, money does not alone control in the new age. Publicity has emerged as a staple. Not traditional news coverage but mere notice, even notoriety. The kind that passes muster if only they spell your name right. The kind that can be ginned up by any performance vivid enough to attract attention.

In this storm of unfiltered noise, a certain kind of candidate can better thrive. They are brazen in exploiting publicity, sometimes for publicity's sake. Newt Gingrich was one of these. Shown to be scorning in personal life the values he preached on the stump, Gingrich simply basked in the extra attention. His faltering presidential run morphed into a thinly disguised book tour.

Donald Trump is another of the sort, with tactics that would make Barnum gag. And the high-octane gall of such campaigns is matched by their cynicism, for the candidates need not care fundamentally about winning. Even a failed presidential candidate can look forward to a lucrative career of political celebrity. Voters who get into bed with such as these may wake in the morning to find themselves alone.

Trump and Gingrich are not the only ones whose campaign style has suggested a cordial awareness of Plan B. Mike Huckabee comes to mind, among others. All have this in common: their tactics telegraph a very low opinion of the voters. Bunco artists depend on the marks' not paying informed attention. Although this is too often true of the American electorate, proper leaders would seek to remedy the circumstance, not to exploit it.

Current Republican candidates cannot be accused of pioneering this low road. Partisan chicanery has been the stock in trade of the national Republican leaders for years. In turning the primaries into a guttersnipes' squabble, this year's candidates have simply taken the model to logical, if sordid, extremes. They have been taught by example that politics is a wildly unprincipled game, even among those who are tasked with governing in the better interest of all the people. And so they've said devil take the hindmost, among their opponents—and among the voters.

Thus, in an odd way, the new information age brings us full circle to speech rights as people's rights, to be used or abused...

Or neglected.

At heart the First Amendments simply means that American citizens may have conversation among themselves without obtaining the government's permission. The notion of conversation necessarily presupposes listening as well as speaking. If free speech is truly to matter, someone must be paying attention. American voters are notorious worldwide for not reliably doing so.

Into the resulting vacuum may step the likes of Trump, redolent of grubby ethics, rapacious self-seeking, feral aggression, and questionable accomplishment. To make headway in today's climate, this sort need not display ability of any kind. They need only be loud and shameless. Trump fits the bill on all counts. Amid Republican bouts of dog-whistle bigotry, he hasn't bothered with the whistle. And consider his caricatures of women and minorities. They are stick-figure crude. They would be laughable were they not so cruel. Even as a bigot, Trump is a stumble-bum.

Yet there he sits, atop the heap. Television newsies—cue the furrowed brow—say voting is heavy. Their cameras show us lines stretching out the polling-place door. And yes, say settled voices, in primary election terms, voting is indeed heavy. On the Republican side, it's the highest since 1980.

And how high is that?

It isn't high. It's pitifully low.

Through the primaries so far, Republican turnout has been 17.3 percent of eligible voters, according to Pew Research. In other words, about 83 percent of eligible voters have not bothered. An even among those who've bestirred themselves, whopping majorities have consistently voted against Trump. But the field is badly splintered, and he manages to do better than any other single candidate. He thrives—so far—by inflaming a minority faction within a minority turnout of a minority party. Neither Trump nor Ted Cruz (let's not leave out the other remaining mountebank) has yet faced anything remotely resembling a fully formed audience, even among Republicans.

Emerging signs suggest that Trump's ranting has backfired by waking the larger electorate early from its traditional primary-season nap. We must hope that the nap habit can be permanently broken. The new information age has sharply elevated the importance of diligent citizenship.

OF SOWING AND REAPING
APRIL 2, 1016

The only thing necessary for the triumph of evil is for good men to do nothing.

Bad laws are the worst sort of tyranny.

—*Edmund Burke*

When I was a youngster, one of my grandmothers had a certain way of praising me to others. She would say, "He's going to be the governor of North Carolina." In her final years, when she lived in a dream world, she would say that I actually *was* the governor of North Carolina. I tried to look gubernatorial in her presence. I couldn't bear any notion of disappointing her.

My grandparents were of the yeoman class who gave this state much of its character. These folks were resourceful in wanting to transcend the worst of Southern history and the systemic poverty of the late nineteenth and early twentieth centuries. City people supported the development of farm-to-market roads for the sake of all. Country people supported a distinguished state university, seeing in it a means for everyone's children to choose a better life. State leaders developed programs to open doors for the poor.

In these and other undertakings, North Carolinians nourished a political ethic that was, by and large, pragmatic and goal-oriented. At key junctures they displayed a shrewd skepticism of labels and ideology. They didn't write the state's official motto, but they could have. It is "Esse Quam Videri"—"To be rather than to seem." They valued leadership. They valued character. My grandmother thought the governor's office should be a pinnacle of both.

I have all this in mind because the leadership of my state has fallen into the hands of low people. One recent development highlights this, for us and for the nation. We now have a law that fosters discrimination on the basis of sexual orientation.

This legalized bigotry is a vividly mean-spirited piece of work. Until the last minute, our legislature handled it behind a cloak of secrecy. Our governor signed it literally in the dark of night. They knew that it couldn't stand scrutiny, and it has in fact created a groundswell of disgust.

If this episode is especially dramatic, it is only one in a shabby pattern. Connivance and dereliction have put our state government in the control of people who give the back of their hand to the long-manifest values of the broader electorate. Our legislature has gone to the outskirts of the Republican right in campaigns heavily underwritten by a wealthy extremist. Along for the well-financed ride was the fellow who became our rookie governor, a pliable wannabe so covetous of office that he has disgraced himself as a public official and as a man.

And where were the rest of us? Asleep at the switch, alas. Complacent about developments in gerrymandered districts where the real elections take place in low-turnout primaries controlled by small minorities of voters. Complacent when the Democratic Party bothered to offer only a cipher as alternative to the bag man's guy for governor. Complacent about the aims of a cohesive faction zealously contemptuous of the values—and the rights—of others.

And so my state must live for a time with the hard lesson that neglect is a stealthy predator on democracy. The nation may be flirting with the same lesson. The Republican Party's presidential nominating process is in the grip of two genuinely bad men who advance by inflaming an emotional minority. Much lament has been focused on their demagoguery. Less has been focused on the statistic for which the United States is notorious among world democracies: 80 percent of the people eligible to vote in the Republican primaries have not bothered. The zealous few have so far controlled the agenda and damaged our country.

In North Carolina, the zealous few have given us leaders who betray their sworn obligation to serve the better interests of all the people. They have tried to deter voting. They have tampered with the university. The list goes on, and it now includes a comprehensive affront to common decency.

Many of us have watched this vandalism with a mixture of outrage and heartache. Genuine citizenship is hard work. Generations of ordinary North Carolinians believed in it and labored at it. They produced government that was clean and diligent. Now, in just a few years, their achievement has been sneered away. It is an epic shame.

A FOGEY'S LAMENT
APRIL 19, 2016

Reflections on the Inevitability of Change in the Human Condition…

Or…

Thoughts on Stuff That Ain't Like It Used to Be, to Wit:

- Bars and barbershops.

I had a soft spot for these. They were havens of a sort, where strangers could josh each other and marvel at the failure of the larger world to align itself with principles radiantly apparent to the patrons of said bars or barbershops.

The barbers were craftsmen. They knew every bump and curve of every head. They knew the eccentricities of every head's owner. A good bartender was said to be the next thing to a priest, and I guess that was about right. But my favorites were the regulars on the customer side of the bar. The ones who always sat in the same places and always had the same agenda. If you wanted conversation, you could talk sports with this one or politics with that one. If you wanted to be left alone, you could sit next to the one who wouldn't speak to you if the earth cracked open.

I don't go to bars much anymore. There seems to be a rule that the walls must be lined with television screens. The barkeep can be seen only in glimpses between the tap handles for fifty different kinds of beer. I've tried. I really have. But I just can't get comfortable with seeing the walls move in my peripheral vision. And who knew that one day the question "What'll you have?" would require an elaborate decision?

Barbershops also have become alien territory. The other day I saw one where the barbers were costumed as sports referees. Being unsure what this was meant to imply about tonsorial skill, I passed on by. Methods have changed as well. Barbers may simply attach an appliance to electric clippers and apply technique they can practice by mowing their lawns. Perhaps this explains why I see young men wearing hairstyles that remind me of cow pies.

Pity.

• Banks.

I understand that business imperatives change. But I do wish that going to the bank didn't make me feel quite so much like a gazelle visiting a pride of lions. The sales pitches are dogged in behalf of services I clearly don't want, because I still don't have them despite the fact that they are pushed on me every time I darken the door.

My bankers are particularly ardent about online banking. The teller always asks me if I do it. I always explain that I prefer not to.

Here, the teller's eyebrows soar. I am convinced that they emphasize this tactic at teller school. In tones one might use to explain that the earth is not flat, the teller assures me that online banking is ever so convenient and absolutely safe and secure. I forbear to say that I have never needed to check my balance at 3:00 a.m. and that believing in foolproof technology is the modern equivalent of believing in unicorns. I simply explain—again—that I am comfortable as I am.

Eventually the teller relents and permits me to approach my own money. I always leave with a feeling that I've disappointed my bank. Time was, my bank would have worried about disappointing me. I liked it that way.

- Language.

With many people, I'm like, you know, totes aggro at the slovenly pidgin that passes for spoken English. Even beyond this I have a special peeve. I hate the use of acronyms in lieu of plain speech.

Perhaps it began with government agencies. Goodness knows they are vigorous exemplars—and can have good reason to cloak their performance in a bit of camouflage. But when did it become a TROUT (a Thing for the Rest of Us Too)?

Now, I suppose we could cut a little slack for Mothers against Drunk Driving and Drug Abuse Resistance Education. The causes are worthy, and the acronyms do make marginally useful sense. (In some quarters, D.A.R.E. stands for Dykes against Racism Everywhere, but perhaps we can agree that this is not general usage.)

Others, in numbers that Google lists in the thousands, are just too cute. Could a bunch of Midwesterners in the beef business be a trade association of some plain sort? Nope. They had to be Cattlemen of Wisconsin.

And speaking of "nope," that word's been hijacked by the National Optimum Population Effort. Just say NOPE!

Peace? That's People Expressing a Concern for Everyone.

And so on.

I think the practice should be outlawed. But given the state of things, not before I have formed the founding chapter of Citizens Raging Against Politicians.

- Instructions and Programming, Part 1

A few years back, I was programming a new gadget. The instructions told me that if I wanted to enable a certain feature, I should go to line 6 on page 8. But there was no line 6 on page 8. There was no line 6 remotely near page 8. I learned to do without that certain feature and, consequently, soon learned to do without the gadget.

Little did I know this was a dark omen for a coming time when everything would have to be programmed. If I'm told someday soon that I must program my trousers, I won't be terribly surprised. And the trouble is, the instructions for our labor-saving devices may be, in my experience, labor-creating devices. They may be opaque. They may be rendered in pictographs too small to make out.

They may be simply dead wrong. Lights may not blink as they are supposed to. Beeps may refuse to beep at the prescribed time. Outright guesswork can be more useful and considerably less stressful.

As one seasoned by time, I have learned to manage the frustration of being buffaloed by electromechanical devices. I have not learned to understand why major companies hire writers who think that grammar, syntax, and accuracy are exotic disciplines.

- Instructions and Programming, Part 2

I have a hankering. It won't go away.

I long for an opportunity to tell the people who program those telephone trees that if I knew my party's extension, I would have dialed it to begin with.

CLOWN PRINCE DONALD
MAY 6, 2016

M y favorite newspaper, *The Washington Post*, says the rise of Donald Trump is "the most repugnant political phenomenon in recent American history." The folks at *The Post* have been in high dudgeon over Trump for a while now. Along with other commentators, they are suffering an acute case of chagrin. According to political rules they thought they knew, this Trump thing wasn't supposed to happen.

By standards in the media world, *The Post* is reasonably good about maintaining arm's length from the people and events it covers. Still, we are all shaped by our environment. The Washington environment is full of political careerists—and political journalists who've reached a professional mecca. Together they make a caste whose members have more in common with each other than with the voters and readers they supposedly serve. Nowadays, these seasoned pros have a particular thing in common: a duplicitous buffoon has put egg on their faces.

And how, in fact, did this happen? The first parts of the answer are voter apathy and vagaries of arithmetic in a Rube Goldberg primary system. Trump gained momentum by running well in a splintered field of crackpots, opportunists, and has-beens. Through March, a steady majority—about 65 percent—voted against him. That is, he "won" primaries with about 35 percent of the votes cast. And 80 percent of those eligible to vote didn't bother.

Even most recently in Indiana, where his majority passed 50 percent, nearly half those who went to the polls voted against him. (And about 3 percent voted for candidates who had long since dropped out of the race. When Chris Christie is finally through in New Jersey, maybe he can get work as a county official in Kokomo.) Turnout data won't be available until May 17, when county election boards have filed their official reports.

Still, results are results. The party of Lincoln is close to nominating a man who exhausts our vocabulary for comprehensive dishonesty. A Trump presidency is extraordinarily unlikely. But we already know that a Trump candidacy is a shame in every sense. If he is the nominee, what follows won't be a proper and useful election campaign. America will be betting national policy on the outcome of a knife fight.

Expert commentators, ever game, say that Trump is destroying the Republican Party. I would say that the party was already well along toward destroying itself, with far-right bigotry and reckless indifference to the principled obligations of high office. In any case, Trump may become clown prince of a political graveyard.

Before the late 1960s, party conventions were the mainstay of candidate selection. But shenanigans discredited the Democratic National Convention of 1968. The climate of attitude turned against decisions made in "smoke-filled rooms." Primary elections gained favor as a more democratic means of choosing nominees.

In this year's menagerie of Republican hopefuls, several set out to exploit an inherent weakness in the primary system. They aimed to succeed by inflaming a cohesive faction. They didn't fear their cynicism would hurt them, because they knew that a whopping majority of voters were not paying attention. With his swindler's ethics, Trump proved to be the best exploiter.

He and the likes of Ted Cruz did not invent the manipulative style of politics, alas. Years of partisan bickering in Congress have held up a vivid model. In it, voters need not be led if only they can be swayed.

Perhaps coming to the brink with this profoundly corrupt man will move leaders and voters toward paying better attention to each other.

DANCING WITH THE DEVIL
JUNE 11, 2016

An old mentor said human organizations can develop an institutional self-interest that conflicts with their supposed purpose. Labor unions were among his examples, along with religious denominations. And, of course, political parties.

In this presidential election year, I'm sure, he would cite the Republican Party for contemplating the nomination of Donald Trump. While time remains for leaders to join the few Republicans who've displayed a gag reflex, the possibility may be remote. Instead, key figures have placed party above country by endorsing Trump. Senate Majority Leader Mitch McConnell tops this list. Close behind is House Speaker Paul Ryan.

Even supposing base motive, one struggles to understand their logic in embracing a walking, talking fraud. And base motive is not an unfair supposition. As leader of an eight-year effort to undermine a duly elected president, McConnell has already shown he is impervious to shame. Ryan staged a brief flirtation with principle but then tried to camouflage travesty by weaseling an endorsement out of the side of his mouth. To put the matter with utmost charity, these are not statesmen.

Both had a chance to redeem themselves when Trump engaged in a prolonged racist rant against a jurist of Mexican descent. Both failed—and did so in revealing fashion. McConnell objected, but not on principle. Rather, he worried that Trump would poison the GOP's relations with Latino voters. Ryan equivocated until the sheer vulgarity of Trump's behavior forced him to call it by name. The message in their behavior? Bigotry is acceptable if you can get away with it politically.

Some experts speculate that McConnell and Ryan see things this way: Opposing Trump would divide the party. This would discourage Republican voters and dampen turnout in the fall. Poor turnout would weaken Republican candidates across the ticket and increase the chances of a Democratic sweep. Thus the incentive to stand united, even behind the likes of Trump.

If this is their thinking, they've disgraced themselves in hopes of short-term partisan gain. And disgrace of this sort is a long-term stain. They've attached their party's reputation—and their own—to one of the lowest figures in American political history. As the twenty-first century electorate moves steadily toward diversity and inclusion, the GOP's leaders are embracing a man who is rabidly hostile to the very concept.

I'm reminded of what another mentor said: People who behave foolishly are apt to be deemed fools. People who exercise power foolishly are apt to be deemed dangerous fools.

GOD AND THE PROSTATE GLAND
JUNE 30, 2016

Recently I ran across a newspaper article that I found quite droll. The writer argued that there is no God. This is not what made his column droll. His premise did: He noted that the male urethra passes through the prostate gland, making it vulnerable in later life to constriction and urinary difficulties. Aha! said the writer. An "intelligent" creator would never have installed such a faulty system. He went on with notions in that vein.

Now, adult males recognize certain Principles for Successful Living. One of them is this: In a public restroom, at halftime of a ball game or a concert, don't get in line behind old guys. I can say from experience that this precept is valid; however, I had never thought to search it for theological import.

And in any case, other anatomical mysteries interest me more. If ever I have the opportunity to quiz the Almighty, I'm going to ask about sinuses. Doubtless my doctor could explain that they serve some purpose. (My doctor can explain a great deal more than he can remedy.) No matter. I simply don't understand why they must occasion so much misery—not to mention the television commercials.

If we think about it in a certain way, God has a pretty good gig. He gets all the credit and none of the blame. He does have to put up with whining about his general failure to abide by standards of human understanding. If he did so, of course, he would be something considerably less than Almighty. In other words, the whining says that God can be God only by agreeing not to be God. This kind of thinking strikes me as being...well, droll.

Nonetheless we persist in efforts to put parameters on deity. At one extreme we have "God is love," at the other "God hates fags." Off to one side, we have my favorite vernacular equivocation: "There ain't necessarily anybody up there, and if there is, he ain't lookin'." This is the spiritual equivalent of going through life shrugging, "Whatever." In youngsters we would call this adolescent ennui. In adults we call it agnosticism.

Some of us claim extra authority in these matters of definition. One is Billy Graham's renegade son Franklin, who apparently considers rage a pastoral skill. On the issue of gay marriage, he rants that proponents are shaking their fists at God. As one of those proponents, I think that we are more nearly shaking our fists at Franklin Graham. Not for the first time, the gentleman seems to be confused about who is Who.

And the kerfuffle goes on. Over on the Christian side of matters, the gospels warn that mere rules are not a means to grace. Meanwhile, major denominations specialize in rulemongering. Pope Francis stirs excitement by declaring that greater room should be made for love. Skeptics say they'll believe he's serious when the Vatican gives all its treasure to the poor and sets up shop in a pole barn.

Here in America, it can be hard to tell the preachers from the politicians. Some of the folks in the pulpit display an appetite for secular power. Some of the pols are ever so glad to have their endorsement. I suppose they would say they are rendering what is Caesar's unto God. They seem indifferent to the risk of rendering what is God's unto Caesar.

Anyhow, what about that newspaper fellow who sees the answer to ultimate questions in his urinary tract? Better writers would here discuss the pitfalls of false syllogism and circular reasoning. My plain-speaking country relatives might simply say that the guy got fascinated with his own cleverness and outsmarted himself.

We do get fascinated with our own cleverness. And when the result is downright silly (see urinary tract, above), maybe we do prove something, in spite of ourselves. Maybe we prove that God enjoys a chuckle now and then.

PRESIDENTIAL ELECTION BLUES
JULY 25, 2016

There's two kinds of people
I just can't stand
An evil-hearted woman
And a lyin' man

—Albert King
"Don't Lie to Me Blues"

When I worked in the newspaper business (my mother never knew; I told her I played piano in a house of ill repute), we did man-on-the-street interviews in election years. We always ran across people who didn't know that a presidential election was being held.

Flash forward to this election year. A sorry truth remains. Even at this point in the season, a great many Americans are only beginning to pay focused attention.

On the Republican side, this has produced the Trump disaster: a comprehensively deceitful bigot with a running mate who would need major improvement to be merely an empty shirt. A huge majority of those eligible to vote in Republican primaries didn't bother. The Republicans left the keys in the car, and it was taken by hooligans.

On the Democratic side, the Clinton candidacy is greeted with enthusiasm by her family, close friends, and people who want to curry favor or get a job. Many more of us—with me among them—are grateful that she is competent but regretful that she brings so much baggage to her candidacy.

Lingering charges of dishonesty seem to me overdone. For decades, foes have labored in vain to prove it against her. True, when caught by the spotlight at awkward junctures, she has sometimes split hairs with the truth. In this she is far from being alone, alas. The habit is endemic in our politics. It is fair to object and to demand better of our leaders in the long term. In the near term, it is not fair and not useful to single her out.

Clinton partisans say she is faulted for traits that would be respected or at least tolerated in a man. They have a point. She can have a hard edge. It hints any given smile may be a pose—or a ruse.

But as the fictional Irish bartender Mr. Dooley used to say, "Politics ain't beanbag." People in positions of power have serious enemies. They forget it at peril to themselves and, more, to their mission. If Clinton keeps an active awareness of this, she is only appropriately armed.

One more problem dogs her. She continues to pay a price for her husband's behavior. She isn't faulted for what he did, at least not by sensible people. Rather, I think, she is the target of a common hunch that she stayed with philandering Bill less for love than for ambition.

Clinton does have one conspicuous shortcoming. She has very little natural gift for the politics of public leadership. She is stiff with the public and graceless as a speaker. Sometimes a president needs to say persuasively to the American people, "Follow me." For a President Hillary Clinton, this would be a challenge. In a Clinton presidency, this would be a material weakness.

With hatemongering and deceit, Donald Trump's campaign will inflict lasting damage on the country. Pundits are saying as well that he has crippled the Republican Party for the long term. This is true in part. However, blame must also be laid to so-called mainstream Republican leaders, who have betrayed the public's trust with eight years of cynical sabotage against a duly elected president.

They are the ones who left the contemporary Republican Party hollow at the core. They are the ones who elevated the example of politics as a trickster's game.

On the assumption that something more useful would emerge, I'd say an implosion in today's Republican Party would be healthy for the country. Meanwhile, we face several dismal months until election day. The blues man Albert King has been dead for a while. Somewhere, perhaps, he is glad that he's not around to be mistaken for a political commentator.

TAKING STOCK OF TAKING STOCK
AUGUST 21, 2016

B ack in a misty yesteryear, someone told me that a wise man pauses now and then to take stock of his life. I don't remember who or where or why. It could have been a mentor, or it could have been a tipsy babbler on the next barstool. For whatever reason, I took the admonition to heart.

Since things have gone pretty well for me in life, I'm usually able to finish taking stock before I finish my first glass of wine. This leaves me feeling derelict in my obligations to wisdom. It also leaves me resentful of the need to invent reasons for having another glass of wine.

But on the assumption that stock-taking techniques, like other skills, benefit from regular exercise, I persist in my efforts. In this way I have long since harvested all the low-hanging fruit, as the cliché goes. I am driven to taking stock of matters that are—I freely admit it—distinctly peripheral.

Thus I recently decided to take stock of all the devices in life that ding, chime, buzz, beep, or whir at me. The list is long. It includes smoke alarms, home security systems, audiovisual devices, and the truck that picks up our garbage.

The kitchen hosts a chorus. The stove and microwave beep when I press their buttons—and beep again if I don't press promptly when they are through. The coffeemaker carries on when it is done, done, done, done, done. The dishwasher does mention that it has finished, but only once. Ding. The refrigerator offers a counterpoint of warbling. It has three voices for dispensing water, crushed ice, or cubed ice.

The kitchen devices are essentially friendly in their attentions to me. As if with a gentle hand on my elbow, they guide me through excursions in nourishment and refreshment. My car, on the other hand, has been given the electronic personality of a scold. It warns me if a seat belt goes even momentarily unfastened. It warns me if it deems that I have backed too close to objects that I can plainly see in my rearview mirrors. If I offer to leave the key behind, it is especially sharp. My car is ever alert for lapses on my part. I imagine a condescending smile in certain shapes on the dashboard.

The ubiquity of these noises has given rise to dubious jokes.

In a grocery store aisle, a portly gentleman is bending over to fetch an item from a bottom shelf. When his cell phone goes off, a little boy exclaims, "Look out Mom, he's backing up!"

It has also caused the princes of technology to develop alternative noises. They've afforded me the option of choosing a cell-phone ringtone that sounds like someone gargling molasses. A while back in our house, a dinner guest's cell phone rang. It just rang. Like a bell. This visibly startled a couple of oldsters in the room, who possibly had not heard a telephone make a simple ringing noise since the days of rotary dials.

In any case, life is what it is. Diligence in adjusting to this reality can make us more complete human beings. I have adjusted to my car's behavior, as I adjusted to the attentions of an autocratic aunt who meant well and didn't realize that she screeched. And I have learned not to fret about the possibility of exhausting even peripheral opportunities to take stock.

I may repeat stock-taking exercises of old. It could be the life-journey equivalent of re-watching a favorite old movie.

Better yet, I could become a consultant of sorts. Offer to take stock of other people's lives. I might even charge a fee. Clients would be expected to pay for my wine, of course.

A CHANCE OF SUNNY RAIN
SEPTEMBER 16, 2016

The shop was not busy, and the guy on the cash register was in a chatty frame of mind. The conversation turned to his college-bound son. He had urged the boy to become a weather forecaster, the guy joked, because they can get things wrong a lot and keep their jobs anyway.

The guy really was joking, and not unkindly. He wasn't setting out to libel an entire profession. Just passing a wry comment on one of life's little quirks and ironies.

And he did have a point, it seems to me. In the morning, when I look out at the emerging day, I do with some regularity have occasion to imagine a chorus of weather forecasters chanting, "Oops!"

We've all had the experience. The snow flurries that turn out to be a blizzard. The rainy day that turns out to be a sunny scorcher. At forecaster school they must talk a lot about learning to try, try again.

And they must talk a lot about learning to talk a lot without actually saying any single thing very clearly. If I pause over the weather reports on television, I hear at length about isobars and fronts. The TV reports have never equipped me to understand them. A front remains, to me, just a squiggly line with little semi-circles sticking out on one side and little triangles sticking out on the other. An isobar is…well, I forget.

I do not hear clearly about the single question that interests me: Is it going to rain tomorrow? When the forecasters finally get around to it, they shroud their answers in a kind of statistical fog. They may say, for example, there is a 20 percent chance of rain. Does this mean a 20 percent chance over 100 percent of the area, or a 100 percent chance over 20 percent of the area? For years I have listened in vain for clarification.

In the interest of fair play, we should stipulate that a certain amount of this is not under the forecasters' control. They are at the mercy of Mother Nature's whims, after all. And in these latter years, they have become slaves to the masters of us all: computers. Watch the weather forecasts long enough, and you'll hear about computer models. In any given weather circumstance, you'll hear about several different computer models. Their diverging forecasts are intended to edify me about all the possibilities. I do understand that. However, I can't help fastening on one thought: the very best-case scenario is that all but one of them are wrong.

Laypeople can develop their own expertise in matters that especially interest them. I have a couple of friends who are football nuts. They are genuinely expert on the game. The same principle applies to those of us who follow weather forecasting. Years of watching it have equipped me to deliver my own weather report on most days.

If the question is: "Will it rain tomorrow?"

A good, serviceable forecast is: "Maybe, maybe not."

Thus my attention to the subject has become more in the nature of a humanitarian enterprise. I imagine a forecaster going home to a spouse who says, "Well, honey, how was your day?" I imagine having to answer that my day consisted of being made to look bad by forces beyond my control.

Thus I am resolved: if I ever meet a forecaster face-to-face, I'm going to make it a point to be especially nice. I suspect they need hugs.

HOW DID TRUMP HAPPEN?
NOVEMBER 9, 2016

As the epochal train wreck of the Donald Trump victory has the world searching for meaning, I am reminded of a story that was much liked by one of my old newspaper colleagues. It concerned a young boy who yearned to be a railroad man.

When he came of age, the boy went straight to the railroad company and applied for a job. "Well," said the manager, "you'll have to take our employment test." The boy did so and then waited in the lobby while the manager graded the result.

"I'm sorry," the manager said when he had finished. "The test says you don't have the aptitude for railroad work. But there's good news. The test results say you'd make a perfect journalist."

"A journalist?" the boy said. "What do you mean?"

"It's in your answer to question number seventeen," the manager said.

"I don't remember the numbers," the boy said. "Which one was that?"

The question was: "What would you do if you were handling the master controls of a railroad switch yard, and you saw two trains hurtling toward each other from opposite directions on the same track?"

The boy's answer was: "I'd run and get my brother, because he's never seen a train wreck."

In the search for meaning, I'm with those who think—for starters—that the press was complicit by dereliction in Trump's rise. My former associates in the fourth estate were too long willing for him to use them as megaphones and too long reluctant to call a toad a toad.

Part of the reason, surely, was simple surprise. We had not before seen this level of barefaced corruption in a presidential nominee. The traditional methods and standards of the press corps were unprepared for it. In the bedrock ethic of the profession, reporting and commentary were to stop somewhere short of participation. If Trump was a ghastly nominee, he was, after all, the nominee. The selection was not up to the press to make.

The impact of surprise was compounded by a time-wrought change in the character of the press itself. Competence has declined. Where once the national press included not a few accomplished students of public affairs, it is now peppered with mere spectators and polemicists. When these don't say much of consequence, it's because they don't have much of consequence to say.

Trump's nomination emerged from a perfect storm of arithmetic happenstance. A substantial majority of Republican primary votes were cast against him. But they were scattered across a splintered and confused field of opponents. A whopping majority of those eligible to vote didn't bother. He took the nomination by winning a fraction of a fraction of the eligible vote.

Yet, in the general election, half the electorate favored him. (We will be amply reminded in the days ahead that half did not.)

Thus the search for meaning: what in the name of sanity were Trump voters thinking?

Some of them were expressing the racial and ethnic bigotry that Trump vigorously stirred, but this cannot be the center-piece of his appeal to a nation that twice elected Barack Obama. Others reflected an aggregation of various single-issue passions. Emblematic might be the evangelical leader who said he was will-ing to accept Trump's ethical sickness as the price of having con-servative Supreme Court nominees.

A portion of blame can be assigned to party-line voting—a convention now carried to such extremes that entire legislative dis-tricts are ceded to one party or another, and elections are little short of sham. With this verdict goes a corollary hunch: Republican loyalists did not feel that Trump's cynical duplicity represented a fundamental departure from established political norms. This view has surely been fed, alas, by years of dereliction in Congress and by two presidential campaigns featuring mercenary, celebrity wannabes masquerading as serious candidates.

A Trump presidency will be a challenge for him as well as the nation—and not only because of his comprehensive incompetence for the job. The bigots and zealots he has energized will be a long time crawling back under their rocks. He will be taxed to sell them on constructive participation in a system whose integrity he him-self has savagely impugned.

The Trump victory will be portrayed by some as a mandate. It is no such thing. It is an aggregation of factors, some of which are cohesively related to each other but many of which share only this moment in history. (He may yet lose the popular vote, and he ran against an historically unpopular opponent.)

Some others will say that this phenomenon should have been impossible in the United States. The founders of our country would shush them. Precisely against such eventualities, they de-signed our system of government to be bigger than any person or party. In particular, it is designed to outlast temporal moods in the electorate. The founders knew that their provisos could someday be needed.

The system remains in our care. Going forward, the quality of our national life will depend on our not flagging in care of it. If we cannot for a time respect our president, we can hold our noses and do citizens' work in respecting, energizing, and enlisting in the rule of law. Today's circumstances have been delivered to us in part by fellow Americans who believed that citizenship could safely be a part-time job.

It can't.

THE COST OF SILENCE
DECEMBER 5, 2016

I n college I had a professor who called himself a Communist. He loved to denounce the American system. That is, he loved to denounce the system that protected his freedom to denounce the system. He thought he was bold and progressive. I thought he was a fuzzy-minded prat.

He would surely be startled to hear me accuse him of being in company with today's fundamentalist right. Beneath cosmetic differences they share a naïve notion: that a system conceived to shelter divergent doctrines would be improved if one doctrine were elevated and empowered to discourage the rest.

Religious fundamentalists aligned with Donald Trump are headed down a rocky road. They have sought to advance their principles by embracing a man who has none. They have imagined that they can safely dance with the devil. With others who have indulged this form of delusion, they will find that the cost is high.

Secular fundamentalists have found a haven for now in the US Congress. This stands as a major irony of the twenty-first century. A great deliberative body has become hostile to honest disagreement. Congress has become a hothouse of absolutism. It has institutionalized intolerance.

That's the genie now loose in American life: the idea that differences among us are inherently disreputable. Racism and homophobia are only two ugly symptoms.

In this climate we arrive at the two big questions facing the nation:

- What is the settled meaning of this presidential election?
- What can we expect from a Trump administration?

To the first question, one offered answer has been that it represents an angry uprising by working-class whites. Although this is certainly an ingredient, it is not the whole recipe of the gumbo. Quite possibly the controlling pronouncement in this election cycle has been not uprising but silence. Trump's nomination was made possible by the huge majority of Republicans who didn't bother to vote in their party's primaries. Hillary Clinton's defeat was made possible by the statistically significant number of Democrats who stayed home in the general election.

In the primaries and in the general election, most of those who actually cast ballots voted against Donald Trump. After he's taken office, will they assert themselves politically? We don't really know. And if all those who remained silent at the ballot box begin to assert themselves politically, what will they assert? We don't really know. The settled meaning of this presidential election very much remains to be seen.

Thus any answer to the second question involves rank speculation. Here's mine: I think there's a lively possibility that what we can expect of a Trump administration is impotence.

He will learn that he cannot govern the country—much less lead the world—with strut and bluster. Any plan B will have to surmount his having made himself an object of widespread fear and ridicule.

He might not have much help in the work. Democrats in Congress likely will replicate the obstructionist tactics refined by Republicans in eight years of working to undermine President Obama. Across the aisle, even the moral dwarfs in leadership may be unable to stomach Trump's capacity for corruption. And in any case, they've long shown they value partisan self-interest above their higher obligations. Partisan self-interest may not include trying to save a manifestly unfit president from himself.

Thus the basics: most of the voters didn't want Trump in the White House, and Congress could have many reasons for being content to let him run in noisy circles.

This melancholy state of affairs won't last, because neither the election of Trump nor the tactical success of the fundamentalist right reflects in any coherent way the character of the American public. The duration will depend on how soon the rest of us realize that if we are not to be ruled by self-interested factions, we must be consistently attentive to the glamourless work of citizenship.

And come to think of it, perhaps that will turn out to be the settled meaning of this election.

ABOUT THE AUTHOR

Stewart T. Spencer worked for forty years as an editor and publisher. He wrote for the *Detroit Free Press,* the *Charlotte Observer,* the *Charlotte News,* and the *Fort Wayne News-Sentinel.* He served as editor in chief for the *Charlotte News* and the *Fort Wayne News-Sentinel.* Under his direction, the *Fort Wayne News-Sentinel* won the Pulitzer Prize in 1983.

Spencer is a proud graduate of Duke University. He is now retired and lives in North Carolina.

www.ingramcontent.com/pod-product-compliance
Lightning Source LLC
Chambersburg PA
CBHW060240290526
45789CB00001B/132